797,885 Books
are available to read at

www.ForgottenBooks.com

Forgotten Books' App
Available for mobile, tablet & eReader

ISBN 978-1-330-00287-2
PIBN 10001246

This book is a reproduction of an important historical work. Forgotten Books uses
state-of-the-art technology to digitally reconstruct the work, preserving the original format
whilst repairing imperfections present in the aged copy. In rare cases, an imperfection in
the original, such as a blemish or missing page, may be replicated in our edition. We do,
however, repair the vast majority of imperfections successfully; any imperfections that
remain are intentionally left to preserve the state of such historical works.

Forgotten Books is a registered trademark of FB &c Ltd.
Copyright © 2015 FB &c Ltd.
FB &c Ltd, Dalton House, 60 Windsor Avenue, London, SW19 2RR.
Company number 08720141. Registered in England and Wales.

For support please visit www.forgottenbooks.com

1 MONTH OF FREE READING

at
www.ForgottenBooks.com

By purchasing this book you are eligible for one month membership to ForgottenBooks.com, giving you unlimited access to our entire collection of over 700,000 titles via our web site and mobile apps.

To claim your free month visit:
www.forgottenbooks.com/free1246

* Offer is valid for 45 days from date of purchase. Terms and conditions apply.

Similar Books Are Available from
www.forgottenbooks.com

An Account of the Manners and Customs of the Modern Egyptians, Vol. 1 of 2
by Edward William Lane

Cults, Customs and Superstitions of India
by John Campbell Oman

Primitive Manners and Customs
by James Anson Farrer

Etiquette for Gentlemen
Or, Short Rules and Reflections for Conduct in Society, by A Gentleman

Totem and Taboo
Resemblances Between the Psychic Lives of Savages and Neurotics, by Sigmund Freud

The Sun and the Serpent
A Contribution to the History of Serpent-Worship, by C. F. Oldham

Etiquette for Americans
by A Woman Of Fashion

An Account of the Manners and Customs of Italy
With Observations, by Giuseppe Marco Antonio Baretti

The Aztecs
Their History, Manners, and Customs, by Lucien Biart

The Bell
Its Origin, History, and Uses, by Alfred Gatty

Bible Manners and Customs
by G. M. Mackie

Chinese Life and Customs
by Paul Carus

Cumberland & Westmorland, Ancient and Modern
The People, Dialect, Superstitions and Customs, by J. Sullivan

Customs and Traditions of Palestine
Illustrating the Manners of the Ancient Hebrews, by Ermete Pierotti

Oriental Customs
by Samuel Burder

Wedding Customs
Then and Now, by Carl Holliday

Dramatic Traditions of the Dark Ages
by Joseph S. Tunison

Hindu Manners, Customs and Ceremonies
by Abbe J. A. Dubois

The Kachins
Their Customs and Traditions, by O. Hanson

Manners, Customs, and Antiquities of the Indians of North and South America
by Samuel G. Goodrich

Photo by George H Davis, Jr.   Courtesy of the *Woman's Home Companion*

READY FOR TEA
The tea table should never be cluttered with a lot of things which the hostess does not need

BOOK OF ETIQUETTE

BY
LILLIAN EICHLER

VOLUME II

—

ILLUSTRATED

NELSON DOUBLEDAY, Inc.
OYSTER BAY, N. Y.
1922

COPYRIGHT, 1921, BY
NELSON DOUBLEDAY, INC.
ALL RIGHTS RESERVED, INCLUDING THAT OF TRANSLATION
INTO FOREIGN LANGUAGES, INCLUDING THE SCANDINAVIAN

PRINTED IN THE UNITED STATES
AT
THE COUNTRY LIFE PRESS, GARDEN CITY, N. Y.

CONTENTS

PART III

CHAPTER   PAGE

I.   SERVANTS   1

The Servant in the Household—A Word to the Mistress—A Word to the Servant—How to Address Servants—The Child and the Servant—The Invisible Barrier—When the Servant Speaks—The Servants of a Big House—The Butler—Correct Dress for the Butler—The Second Man—The Chauffeur—Duties of the Chauffeur—The Valet—The Page—The Maid-Servants—Lady's Maid—The Nurse-Maid—Duties of House-Maid—In Conclusion.

II.   DINNERS   23

About the American Hostess—Planning the Formal Dinner — Arranging the Table — Starting at the Center—Some Important Details—Table Etiquette—Table Service—Use of the Napkin—The Spoon at the Dinner Table—The Fork and Knife—Finger Foods — Table Accidents — The Hostess — When the Guests Arrive—The Successful Hostess—The Guest—Comments on Food—Second Helpings—The Menu—Special Entertainment—When to Leave—Taking Leave —Inviting a Stop-Gap—Simple Dinners—Inviting Congenial Guests—When There are no Servants—Hotel Dinners—Dress for Dinner.

CONTENTS

CHAPTER   PAGE

III. LUNCHEONS 48

Purpose of the Luncheon—Informal Luncheons—About the Table—The Formal Luncheon—The Table for the Formal Luncheon—Hostess and Guest—Formal and Informal Breakfasts—Dress for Luncheons and Breakfasts.

IV. TEAS AND OTHER ENTERTAINMENTS 56

Evolution of the Afternoon Tea — The Simpler Tea—The Formal Tea—The Tea-Table—Dress at Tea Time—The Garden Party—Receiving the Guests—On the Lawn—Dress for Garden Parties and Lawn Festivals—Woman's Garden Costume—The Man at the Garden Party—House Parties—Sending the Invitation—When the Guests Arrive—Entertaining at the House Party—Hostess and Guests at the House Party—"Tipping" the Servants.

V. WHEN THE BACHELOR ENTERTAINS 76

When the Bachelor is Host—Welcoming the Guests—The Bachelor's Dinner—Tea at a Bachelor Apartment—The Bachelor Dance—Theater Parties—Yachting Parties.

VI. MUSICALES AND PRIVATE THEATRICALS . . . 83

Preparations for the Musicale—The Afternoon Musicale — The Evening Musicale — Card Parties at the Musicale—Duties of Guests at Musicales—Dress at the Musicale—Arranging Private Theatricals—The Players—The Guests—Host and Hostess.

VII. DANCING 91

Dancing as a Healthful Art—Dance-Giving No Longer a Luxury—The Début Dance—

CONTENTS

vii

CHAPTER

PAGE

Costume Balls—Subscription Dances—The Ballroom—Music at the Dance—Dance Programs—Dinner Dances—Dressing Rooms— The Dance—When the Lady is Asked to Dance—"Cutting In"—Dancing Positions— When the Guest Does Not Dance—Public Dances—A Plea for Dancing—The Charm of Dress in Dancing—At the Afternoon Dance—Gentlemen at the Dance—Dress for the Ball — Dress of the Débutante — Wraps at the Ball—Ball Dress for Men—For the Simple Country Dance.

VIII. GAMES AND SPORTS 114
Why the World Plays—Fair Play—Indoor Games — Chess — Bridge — Billiards and Croquet—Outdoor Games—Lawn Tennis— Golf—Some Important Rules about Golf— Football—Automobile Etiquette—Automobile Parties—Riding—Bathing—Sports—Clothes in General.

PART IV

I. SPEECH 135
Conversation — The Charm of Correct Speech—Courtesy in Conversation — The Voice—Ease in Speech—Local Phrases and Mannerisms—Importance of Vocabulary— Interrupting the Speech of Others—Tact in Conversation—Some Important Information —What to Talk About.

II. DRESS 147
The First Impression — Men's Dress — Women's Dress—The Story of Dress—The Dawn of Fashion—The Fashions of To-day

viii CONTENTS

CHAPTER   PAGE

—Harmony in Dress—Importance of Color —The Charm of Personality — Gaudiness versus Good Taste — "Extravagance the Greatest Vulgarity" — Inappropriateness in Clothes—The Eccentric Dresser—Comfort in Clothes—If One is Not Average—Tall and Short People—The Well-Dressed Woman— Not a Slave to Fashion—The Well-Dressed Man—The Charm of Old Age—The Elderly Woman—Imitation and Over-Dressing—The Older Gentleman—A Trip to the South—For the Gentleman.

III. THE BUSINESS WOMAN 177

Woman in the Business World—Self-Confidence—The Slattern—Following the Fashions—Gaudy Attraction—The Business Suit —The Business Dress and Coat—An Appeal to Business Women.

IV. ON THE STREET 185

The True Etiquette—Poise in Public—The Charm of Courtesy—Ladies and Gentlemen —When to Bow in Public—Walking in Public—Stopping for a Chat—When Accidents Happen—Accepting Courtesies from Strangers—Raising the Hat—How to Raise the Hat—In the Street Car—Entering the Car —In the Taxicab—Some Social Errors.

V. AT THE THEATER AND THE OPERA 201

Dress at the Theater and Opera—Entering the Theater—Arriving Late—About Wraps —Order of Precedence—Before the Play— When the Curtain is Drawn—During the Performance — The Offending Hat — Applause—During Intermission—Leaving the Theater.

CONTENTS

CHAPTER		PAGE
VI.	HOTEL ETIQUETTE	210

At the Hotel—The Woman Guest—Receiving Masculine Guests—Making Friends at the Hotel—How to Register—In the Public Dining-Room—Hotel Stationery—Regarding the Servants—Leaving the Hotel.

VII.	TRAVEL ETIQUETTE	219

The Restless Urge of Travel—The Customs of Countries—The Traveler's Wardrobe—In the Train—In the Sleeping Car—Train Courtesy — The Woman Traveler — The Woman who Travels with an Escort—In the Dining-Car—Children on the Train—In the Taxicab—Bon Voyage Gifts—On Board the Ship—Courtesy of the Ship—The Woman Crossing the Ocean—A Concert at Sea—At the Journey's End—At Hotel and Restaurant—At Tea-Room and Roof-Garden—To Those Who Love to Travel.

VIII.	TIPPING	237

An Un-American Custom—Lavish Tipping—In Dining-Room or Dining-Car—At the Hotel—The Taxi-Driver—On the Train—Crossing the Ocean—Tips in Foreign Countries.

IX.	ETIQUETTE ABROAD	244

The American in Foreign Countries—On English Soil — Addressing Royalty — Other English Titles—And Still Other Titles—Addressing Clergy Abroad—Lawyers, Statesmen and Officials—How to Address Them—At the Court of England—What to Wear to Court—The King's Levees—In France—Addressing Titled People in France—Certain

CONTENTS

PAGE

French Conventions — Dinner Etiquette — French Wedding Etiquette — Balls — About Calls and Cards — Correspondence — The American in Germany—The Perfect American Tourist.

APPENDIX 265

Foreign Words in Frequent Social Usage.

LIST OF ILLUSTRATIONS

READY FOR TEA . . . . *Frontispiece*

PAGE

TABLE SET FOR DINNER 32

THE PUNCH TABLE 112

THE BUFFET LUNCH 208

PART III

Repose and cheerfulness are the badge of the gentleman,—repose in energy. The Greek battle pieces are calm; the heroes, in whatever violent actions engaged, retain a serene aspect; as we say of Niagara, that it falls without speed. A cheerful, intelligent face is the end of culture, and success enough. For it indicates the purpose of nature and wisdom attained.

—Emerson.

CHAPTER I

SERVANTS

THE SERVANT IN THE HOUSEHOLD

"A mouse can look at a king, but a king won't often look at a mouse" says the old proverb. Which is, sadly enough, the state of affairs between servants and mistresses in many households.

A great many people feel somehow that those who labor in the capacity of servants are inferior. But in most cases, it is those who place servants on a lower plane who are themselves inferior. We owe those who take a part in the household affairs of our homes, more than the wages we pay them. We owe them gratitude, courtesy, kindness. Many elaborate dinners would be failures if it were not for the silent members of our households. Many formal entertainments would be impossible without their help. They hold a certain place of importance in the home—and it should be recognized in the social world as a place worthy of every courtesy and respect.

For those who are fortunate enough to have servants to help with domestic tasks, it is extremely important that the correct etiquette of servants be thoroughly known and understood. And those who serve as butlers and maids and valets must also know the little rules of good conduct that govern their duties and responsibilities. The information contained in the following paragraphs is meant for

BOOK OF ETIQUETTE

both the servant and the mistress, and we hope that both will find it valuable.

A WORD TO THE MISTRESS

In the home where guests are frequently entertained and where the hostess holds many formal social functions, servants are essential.

Every family that can afford to do so, should have one, or two, or more servants according to social requirements and the appointments of the house. They should be well instructed in their duties and they should be expected to carry them out faultlessly. Untidy, noisy, ill-trained servants reflect upon the manners and conduct of the mistress herself.

The most common method of engaging a servant is through an agency. Here different types of men and women can be found, and the mistress of the household may be fortunate enough to find one suited to her requirements. Sometimes she secures a maid or butler by the recommendation of some other housekeeper. This method is usually more satisfactory than any other because it puts things on a rather friendly basis from the start.

But whether the maid or butler be engaged by recommendation or through an agency, it is important that it be clearly understood from the beginning just what his or her duties will be. And the mistress should not engage a servant unless she feels sure that he will be able to fill the position satisfactorily, for it is both an expensive and provoking process to change servants frequently.

The first few days in a new home are always difficult for the servant. The mistress should be patient and considerate and do all she can to make the newcomer feel at ease

SERVANTS

in her new surroundings. Her directions should be requests, not commands, and she should overlook blunders
for they may be the result of the servant's unfamiliarity
with the household and its customs.

After the servant has been in the household three weeks
or a month, the mistress has every right to expect him to
carry out his duties correctly. But we are all human, and
we all make mistakes. When a servant blunders through
carelessness a reprimand may be necessary, but to scold
in loud, angry tones is most ill-mannered. The well-bred
woman will never forget that there is as much demand for
courtesy and kindliness in her relations with her servants
as in any other relation in which she is placed. There is
absolutely no reason why "please" and "thank you" should
be omitted when we speak to the people who live in our
homes and labor for our comfort and happiness.

A WORD TO THE SERVANT

Among real Americans, with their democratic views,
there can be no objection to the word "servant." It is a
noun, a name, to denote people in a certain occupation;
just as "brokers" and "salesmen" and "housewives" denote certain people in other occupations. Therefore the
servants who read these sentences, and the women who
have servants in their households, should interpret the
word in the spirit it is written—that of true American
courtesy and respect.

Domestic service requires a certain character lacking
in most other professions. As a servant, you care for the
things of others and it should be done with as much attention and regard as if they were your own. You attend
to your duties day after day, persisting in work which

BOOK OF ETIQUETTE

may sometimes become monotonous and which would be easy enough to shirk, but which you do for the comfort and pleasure of your mistress. You find yourself in the position of keeping other people's property attractive, putting other people's visitors at ease and being economical with other people's money. And we repeat again that it requires a certain high stamp of character that is not found in most professions.

Tidiness is very important in both men and women servants. The maid who serves at the dinner table must wear a fresh new blouse and a crisp apron. Soiled finger-nails or unclean hands are inexcusable. The well-trained servant presents always an immaculate, well-groomed appearance.

It hardly seems necessary to mention that the servant must be scrupulously honest. Perhaps, in their capacity in the home, they are exposed to unusual temptations— but that is just the reason why they should refrain from dishonesty of any kind, even the slightest lie. Gossip about the family life of the people they are serving should also be avoided by servants.

The servant should remember that whether she be maid or mistress, she can be *cultured*. The well-bred, well-trained maid is never sullen or perverse. Nor is her manner servile or haughty. She is respectful to her employers, but she does not cringe. She does her duties carefully, conscientiously and thoroughly, and she carries out the commands of her mistress without question. If, however, a maid thinks that a certain task could be done much more quickly and satisfactorily in another way, she may suggest it to her mistress and request her permission to do it in that way. If she is reprimanded for a mistake, she should not become rude or angry, but remain calm and answer

SERVANTS

5

quietly. It will not be long before her mistress, if she is the right sort of mistress, recognizes her superior qualities, her good manners and conscientious work, and will respond by treating her in like manner.

Undue familiarity from the maid is not to be countenanced. But many times a certain understanding friendliness develops between a faithful maid and a kind and courteous mistress—a friendship in which rigid class distinctions are not sufficient to form a barrier.

Let those of us who are servants remember that it is only in helping others that true happiness is found, and that the world is quick to recognize and reward true, loyal, sincere service.

HOW TO ADDRESS SERVANTS

Household servants are usually addressed by their first names. It is indeed bad form to address a servant by some abbreviated nickname, such as Lizzy for Elizabeth or Maggie for Margaret. The full first name should be used. A pleasant "Good morning, Margaret," starts the day right, both for the mistress and the maid. In England the surname is preferred but they do not have to contend with all the foreign importations in the way of names that we have here in America. It is certainly better to call John Soennichsen John, than to use his surname.

A butler or chauffeur is usually addressed by his surname unless he is a man who has served the family for many years.

The golden rule of "Thank you" is just as golden when it applies to our servants. It is only the extremely discourteous man or woman who will address servants in a peremptory, rude tone. And it is especially ill-bred and

6　　BOOK OF ETIQUETTE

unkind to be overbearing to servants in the presence of guests, or to scold one servant in the presence of another.

THE CHILD AND THE SERVANT

Insolence to servants on the part of children is as much a reflection on the manners of the parents, as it is upon the breeding of the children. The child that hears the servants addressed in rude, haughty manner will quite naturally adopt the same manner towards them. And no one, child or adult, can be considered well-bred unless he or she is courteous and kind to everyone, especially to those whose social position is inferior.

In the park, recently, a little tot of six years or thereabouts had a bag of peanuts which she offered to two little playmates and also to their mother who was sitting near by. Seeing that she did not offer her governess some peanuts, the woman inquired, "Why don't you offer Miss Taylor some?" To which the youngster immediately replied, "Oh, she's only my governess."

This is the result of wrong principle in the home. No child is born a snob. No child is born haughty and arrogant. It is the home environment and the precedent of the parents that makes such vain, unkind little children as the one mentioned above. It is actually unfair to the young children in the home to set the wrong example by being discourteous to the servants. They will only have to fight, later, to conquer the petty snobbishness that stands between them and their entrance into good society.

THE INVISIBLE BARRIER

In the sixteenth century French women servants were arrested and placed in prison for wearing clothes similar

SERVANTS

to those worn by their "superiors." It developed that they had made the garments themselves, copying them from the original models, sometimes sitting up all night to finish the garment. But the court ruled that it made no difference whether they had made them themselves or not; they had worn clothes like their mistresses', and they must be punished! We very much wiser people of the twentieth century smile when we read of these ridiculous edicts of a long-ago court—but we placidly continue to condemn the shop-girl and the working-girl if she dares to imitate Parisienne importations.

It is very often the same in the household. We ridicule the "class systems" of other countries, yet we deliberately build up a barrier between ourselves and those who work for us. Perhaps there must be some such barrier to keep the social equilibrium; but is there any reason why it should be unkind and discourteous?

The mistress should not, of course, confide in her servants, gossip with them, discuss her affairs with them, enter their quarrels and take sides with them. But she can be cheerful, polite, considerate; and invariably she will find that this kind of treatment will bring an immediate response—even from the most sullen servant.

WHEN THE SERVANT SPEAKS

In answering the mistress or master of the household, it is customary for the servant to say, "Yes, madam," or, "Yes, sir." Old servants, who have been for many years in the employ of the same people, may omit the "madam" and use the name, in this manner,—"Yes, Mrs. Brown." Such slovenly expressions as "No'm" or "Yessir" show

BOOK OF ETIQUETTE

lack of good training on the part of the servant, and poor judgment on the part of the mistress.

Brevity and civility are the two most important virtues of the speech of the man or maid servant who answers inquiries at the door, admits guests and takes messages. In the latter case, when a servant takes a message for one of the members of the household, a polite "Thank you, madam" is essential. If there is a doubt as to whether or not the hostess is at home, the well-trained servant admits the visitor, asks her to have a seat, and says, "I will inquire." He returns to say either that Madam is not at home, or that she will be down directly.

When announcing guests, the butler should ask, "What name, please?" not in the indifferent, sing-song manner so characteristic of butlers, but in a cordial, polite tone of voice, and with a genial smile. Having been given the names of the visitors, he announces them in clear, distinct tones. These announcements are made while the guests are entering the drawing-room. A mother and two daughters are announced as: "Mrs. Smith, the Misses Smith." If the given names of the young ladies are called, the form of announcement is: "Mrs. Smith, Miss Smith, Miss Alice Smith," the eldest daughter of a family being given the privilege to use the title "Miss Smith." In announcing a gentleman and his son, the butler says: "Mr. Blank, Mr. Francis Blank."

THE SERVANTS OF A BIG HOUSE

The small household must choose servants according to convenience and requirements. Where there are three or four grown-up daughters and the home is a small one, one maid and one butler are sufficient. But in a very large

SERVANTS

house with numerous rooms, where many social functions are held and many house parties are given by the hostess a full corps of servants is required. Each one should have certain, definite tasks to perform every day.

In the luxurious American home, seven servants are usually employed. They are a butler, a chauffeur, a parlor maid, a cook, a laundress, a nurse-maid and a chambermaid. A lady's maid and a valet are sometimes added. A footman, laundry-maid and scullery-maid are also added, sometimes, to the corps of servants. But this list may be increased or diminished according to the requirements of the individual family. For instance, a second-man may be placed under the direction of the butler; a gardener and his assistants may be charged with the care of the environs; while grooms may be employed to care for the horses in the stables. But usually these additional servants are the luxuries of the extremely wealthy and should not be indulged in by those who cannot afford them.

In the home where there are several men servants and several women servants, it is the best plan for the wife to supervise the duties and responsibilities of the women, leaving the men to be directed by her husband. It is important, though, for the mistress of the house not to give counter commands to servants who are under her husband's supervision, for this may cause a friction that is not conducive to the best service on the part of the help.

THE BUTLER

The duties of the butler confine him to the drawing-room and dining-room. The dining-room, however, is his

BOOK OF ETIQUETTE

particular domain; he sees that everything is in order, that the table is laid correctly, the lighting effect satisfactory, the flowers arranged, and in short that the room and appointments are in perfect readiness for a punctual meal. In this work a parlor maid assists him by sweeping and dusting, and a pantry-maid helps him by keeping everything immaculate and in readiness in the pantry.

The butler serves at breakfast, luncheon and dinner. Where there is a second-man, he may assist the butler with the serving at dinner; and at large entertainments the maid who assists in the pantry may also be requested to serve. The butler also is in charge of the afternoon-tea duties, in homes where this custom prevails. He brings in the tray, arranges it for the hostess and sees that everyone is served.

Where there are only a few servants, the butler may be expected to help with the dishes, polish the silver and assist in the pantry. But if there are maid servants, and a second-man to do the heavier work, then he is expected to serve in a small measure as the valet for the master of the house. He lays out his evening clothes, brushes and presses the garments worn in the morning, and draws his bath. Sometimes, when his domestic duties are very light, the butler is requested to serve as footman to the mistress when she goes riding in the afternoon.

An important duty of the butler is to answer the door bell whenever it rings. He must see that the front door and the hall is in order and well-swept, and that the drawing-room door is locked every night after the family has retired. A great deal of the comfort and pleasure of the family depends upon the manner in which the butler attends to his duties.

SERVANTS

CORRECT DRESS FOR THE BUTLER

Neatness of attire is extremely important. The butler should be clean-shaven, and he should not fail to be fresh-shaven every day. His hair should not be closely cropped, but cut loosely, and it should be well-brushed at all times. Well-kept nails are, of course, very important not only for the butler but for anyone who serves at the table or has anything to do with the food.

As nearly as possible, the butler's costume should parallel the following description, but each passing season finds some minor detail slightly changed, and each new season finds a slight variation from the costume of the season before. So the best thing to do is to find out definitely from a reliable clothier or from the men's furnishing department of a large department store, just what the butler's costume of the present time consists of.

Ordinarily, the butler wears white linen in the morning, with black or dark gray trousers, a black waistcoast that buttons high, and a swallow-tail coat. It is also permissible for him to wear a short roundtail coat in the morning hours; it is similar to the gentleman's tailless evening coat, but it is not faced with silk. A black or dark tie and black shoes complete the outfit, which is worn until after the midday meal.

If guests are to be entertained at luncheon, the butler wears his afternoon and evening livery. Otherwise he dons it only after luncheon or about three o'clock in the afternoon. It consists of complete black evening dress similar in cut and style to that worn by gentlemen. There are no braidings or facings, though the material of the suit may be every whit as excellent in quality as that worn by the

BOOK OF ETIQUETTE

master of the house. The butler does not wear a white waistcoat, a watch chain, or jeweled studs with his afternoon or evening livery. Nor may he wear a *boutonnière* or an assertive tie or patent leather shoes. And it is extremely bad taste for him to use perfume of any kind. He wears white linen with plain white studs in the shirt front, a standing collar, white lawn tie and plain black shoes. His watch is slipped into his waistcoast pocket without chain or fob.

White gloves are no longer the custom for men servants in the private home.

When acting as footman to his mistress in the afternoon, the butler wears the livery described for the second man. In cold weather he is supplied with a long footman's coat; and he is also supplied with a top hat and gloves, all matching in color and style those worn by the chauffeur.

THE SECOND MAN

The second man may be employed exclusively for the house, or he may be employed solely to serve as footman, sitting next to the chauffeur when the mistress is motoring. In the latter case he wears the regular livery matching that worn by the chauffeur. But usually a second man is expected to help in the house besides serving as footman.

He assists the butler by answering the door bell whenever the other is busy or occupied elsewhere. He washes dishes and windows and polishes the silver. He tends to the open fireplace in winter, and to the arranging of the flowers in the summer. The veranda, front steps and courtyard are also in his care. And when there are guests

SERVANTS

for dinner, or at a large entertainment, he helps serve at the table.

The livery of the second man is the same indoors all day; he does not change for the evening. It consists of coat and trousers of one solid color determined by the heads of the house. It is usually a very dark green, brown, gray or blue, and the outside edge of the trouser leg is piped in some contrasting color. The coat is usually swallow-tail in cut, and is ornamented with brass or silver buttons on the tails, on the cuffs and down the front. Lately this vogue of the brass and silver button is disappearing.

The color worn by the second man should be the predominating color worn by all the other liveried servants in the household. It is certainly not good form to have the chauffeur wear one color of livery, and the footman next to him wear livery of an entirely different color and cut. With his livery described above, the second man wears a waistcoat of Valencia, striped in the two colors that appear on the coat and trousers. It is usually cut V shape, disclosing white linen in which are fastened two plain white studs, a standing collar, and a white lawn tie. When he serves as footman, the second man may either be requested to don complete car livery, or he may wear a long footman's overcoat, top hat and gloves over his house livery.

A clean shaven face and well-brushed, close-clipped hair are pleasing characteristics of the second man. Untidiness, ill-kept hands and nails, and the use of jewelry or perfume should not be tolerated in the second man, whether he serves only as footman, or in the house. When he helps the butler at the dinner table, he should be especially immaculate in appearance.

BOOK OF ETIQUETTE

THE CHAUFFEUR

The gallant coachman of a decade ago has given way to the chauffeur of to-day. But we find that his livery is no less important—it is governed by a very definite convention.

In winter, for instance, the chauffeur wears long trousers of melton or kersey or similar material and a double-breasted greatcoat of the same material. The collar and cuffs may be of a contrasting color or of the same color as the rest of the material. He wears a flat cap with a stiff visor and a band of the same contrasting color that appears on the collar and cuffs of the coat. Dark gloves and shoes are worn. Sometimes, instead of long trousers, the chauffeur wears knee-trousers with leather leggings. If desired, a double row of brass, silver or polished horn buttons may decorate the front of the greatcoat, but this must be determined by the prevailing custom. If the weather is extremely cold, the chauffeur should be provided with a long coat of goat or wolf-skin, or some other suitable protection against the cold and wind.

During the summer months, the chauffeur usually wears gray or brown cords, developed in the conventional style. His cap and gloves match.

DUTIES OF THE CHAUFFEUR

The complete care of the car or cars devolves upon the chauffeur. He must see that it is always spotless and shining, that it is in good condition and will not break down during a trip, and that it is in readiness whenever the owners want to use it.

When the mistress goes motoring, the chauffeur stands

SERVANTS

at the door of the car until she enters, arranges the robes and sees that she is comfortable before taking his own place. Upon receiving her orders, he touches the rim of his cap. It is not necessary, however, upon reaching the destination for the chauffeur to descend and open the door for his mistress. His place is at the wheel and that is where he remains. But if there is a second man to assist the chauffeur, who accompanies him on every trip as a motor footman, he should descend and stand at attention while the mistress emerges from the car.

The footman dresses like the chauffeur. He leaves cards when the mistress makes her social calls, and he rings house bells for her. He is also expected to be useful in performing personal service for the masculine members of the household.

Very often it happens that a tourist, instead of hiring a car and chauffeur when he reaches a strange country, desires to take his own car and chauffeur with him. He must be sure to arrange beforehand to have the man admitted to the foreign country, for negligence may cause him much delay and trouble when he reaches the border-line. He must also arrange for the sleeping and eating facilities of his chauffeur when they stop for a day or two in a town or village. It is not right to expect him to eat with the servants, nor will he wish to eat at the same table with his employer. It is wisest to give him an allowance and permit him to eat and sleep where he pleases.

THE VALET

The business of the valet is to attend to all the comforts and desires of the master of the house. He takes no part in the general housework, except in an emergency.

BOOK OF ETIQUETTE

The valet does not wear livery. Indoors, in the evening and during the day, he wears dark gray or black trousers, white linen, a high-buttoned black waistcoat and a plain black swallow-tailed coat or one cut with short rounded tails. He wears a dark tie and dull leather shoes. He may also wear an inconspicuous pin in his tie and simple cuff-links; but a display of jewelry is not permissible.

It may happen that a butler is ill or called away, or that there is a shortage of servants during a large entertainment. In this case the valet may be called upon to serve as a butler, and he then wears complete butler's dress, with the long-tailed coat. When traveling with his employer, the valet wears an inconspicuous morning suit of dark gray, brown or blue tweed in the conventional style. He completes this outfit with a black or brown derby hat and black leather shoes.

The duties of the valet are as follows: he brushes, presses, cleans, packs or lays out the clothes of his employer, draws the water for his bath, and assists him to dress. He keeps his wardrobe in order and packs and unpacks his trunks whenever he is traveling. He does all his errands, buys his railway and steamship tickets, pays his bills, and carries his hand-luggage when they are traveling together. Sometimes he shaves him, orders his clothes, and writes his business letters. But these duties are expected only of accomplished valets. He does not, however, make the bed or sweep or dust his employer's room.

THE PAGE

The page is a very convenient servant to have when there is no second-man or when there are no men-servants at all. His duties are many and varied. He runs errands

SERVANTS

17

for everyone in the house, assists the parlor-maid, looks after the open fire places and opens the door to callers. Sometimes he even serves as a sort of miniature footman, sitting next to the chauffeur in complete footman livery.

The livery for the page boy is the same during the day and evening. It is a simple, neat coat and trousers of dark cloth piped with the contrasting livery color of the family in which he serves. The coat fits the body snugly, and ends at the waistline except for a slight point at back and front. Metal buttons set as closely together as possible fasten the coat from top to bottom. The trousers are piped or braided in the contrasting color down the outside of the leg. White linen should show at the wrists and above the high collar of the coat, but there should be no tie. Black calf skin shoes complete the outfit, and when the page is out of doors, he wears a round cap to match his suit.

The bullet-shaped metal buttons down the front of the coat, and three of the same buttons sewed on the outside seam of the cuffs, have earned for the page the rather appropriate name of "Buttons."

THE MAID-SERVANTS

Whether there is only one maid-servant in the house, or many, their duties should be clearly defined and understood. It is the only way to avoid quarreling and misunderstanding among the servants themselves. Let each one understand from the very first day he begins work just what his duties are. In this case as in many another an ounce of prevention is worth a pound of cure. If there are quarrels among the servants the mistress should not interfere nor take sides. If possible she should remove

BOOK OF ETIQUETTE

the cause of the friction, and for a serious fault she should discharge the one that is causing the disturbance.

The services of the waitress are confined to the drawing-room floor. She serves breakfast, luncheon and dinner, and afternoon tea where it is the custom. This is assuming, however, that there is no butler in the home. In this case she attends to all the other duties that would ordinarily fall upon him. She answers the door-bell, polishes the silver, helps with the washing of the dishes and sees that the table is correctly laid for each meal.

The parlor maid is a luxury enjoyed only by families of great wealth. She is expected to devote her time and attention wholly to the drawing-room and dining-room, assisting the waitress in the pantry and keeping the library and drawing-room in order. But in the average comfortable home of America there are usually only two maids, a housemaid and a waitress (with perhaps the additional services of a cook) and these two maids have the care of the dining, living and bedrooms divided between them.

The dress of the house-maids is very much alike. The waitress, or parlor maid, wears a plain, light-colored dress in the morning with a rather large apron, and a small white cap. The chambermaid's costume is very much the same. In the afternoon the parlor maid or waitress changes to a black serge dress in winter, or a black poplin in summer, with white linen cuffs and collars and a small white apron.* (See footnote.)

The maid-servants never wear jewelry or other finery

---

* The costumes for maid-servants change frequently, only in slight details, but enough to warrant specific research at the time the servant is outfitted. A large department store, or a store devoted exclusively to the liveries of servants, will be able to tell you exactly the correct costumes for maid-servants at the present time. Or you may find the desired information in a current housekeeping magazine.

SERVANTS

19

while they are on duty. One very simple brooch, or perhaps a pair of cuff links, is permissible; but bracelets, rings and neck ornaments are in bad taste. Elaborate dressing of the hair should also be avoided, and careless, untidy dressing should never be countenanced.

LADY'S MAID

The lady's maid does not take part in the general housework. Her duties are solely to care for the wardrobe of her mistress, to assist her at her toilette, to draw her bath, to lay out her clothes and keep her room tidy. But she does not sweep or dust the room or make the bed—these are the duties of the chamber-maid. If she is an accomplished maid she will probably do a great deal of sewing, and perhaps she will massage her mistress' hair and manicure her nails. But these duties are not to be expected; the mistress who finds her maid is willing to do these things for her, is indeed fortunate.

A black dress in winter, and a black skirt and waist in summer, worn with a small, dainty white apron comprises the costume of the lady's maid. Stiff white cuffs and collar add a touch of prim neatness which is most desirable. At the present time, the tiny white cap formerly worn by lady's maids has been almost entirely dispensed with.

When traveling with her mistress, the lady's maid should wear only very simple and inconspicuous clothes. A tweed suit worn with a neat blouse, or a tweed coat worn over a simple dress, is the best form. Anything gaudy or elaborate worn by a lady's maid is frowned upon by polite society.

BOOK OF ETIQUETTE

THE NURSE-MAID

The nurse-maid should be very particular about her dress. She should always be faultlessly attired, her hair neat and well-brushed, her entire appearance displaying a tidy cleanliness.

In the house the nurse-maid wears a simple dress of wool or heavy material with a white apron and white collar and cuffs. In warmer weather she wears linen or poplin with the apron and collar and cuffs. Outdoors, she wears a long full cloak over her house dress.

DUTIES OF HOUSE-MAID

The cook, who is always dressed spotlessly in white, does nothing outside the kitchen unless special arrangements have been made to the contrary. She keeps the kitchen tidy and clean, cooks the meals, helps with the dishes and perhaps attends to the furnace.

The waitress opens and airs the living-rooms, dusts the rooms and gets everything in readiness for breakfast. It is customary to excuse her as soon as the principal part of the breakfast has been served, so that she may attend to her chamber-work and be ready to come down to her breakfast by the time the family has finished. However, before she goes to her own breakfast, she is expected to clear the dining-room table and take the dishes into the kitchen.

If the waitress does not help with the chamber-work, this duty falls entirely upon the chamber-maid. She must make the beds, sweep and dust the bedrooms, and keep them immaculate. The mistress should inspect the cham-

SERVANTS

ber-work occasionally for servants must not be permitted to feel that carelessness in details will be overlooked. And the mistress should also take care of her own linen-closet, unless she has a very trustworthy and competent servant; for linens should be worn alike, and not some worn constantly and others allowed to lie forgotten in a corner of the closet.

IN CONCLUSION

A good servant—and by "good" we mean a man or woman who goes about duties cheerfully, is respectful and willing, who is neat, well-mannered and well-trained— must be treated in the right manner if he or she is to remain such. There are so many blunders the mistress can make, so many mistakes that bring the wrong response from those who are temporarily a part of her household.

For instance, a haughty, arrogant manner towards a servant who is sensitive will by no means encourage that servant to do his or her best work. And on the other hand, a servile manner towards a good servant one is afraid of losing, encourages that servant to take liberties and become unduly familiar.

It is as difficult to be a good mistress as it is to be a good servant. Both duties require a keen understanding and appreciation of human nature, a kindliness of spirit and a desire to be helpful. Both the servant and the mistress have their trials and troubles, but they should remember that it is only through mutual helpfulness and consideration, an exacting attention to duties and responsibilities, a wise supervision and a faithful service, that harmony and happiness can be reached in the home. And both should bear in mind that this harmony and happi-

BOOK OF ETIQUETTE

ness is something worth-while striving for, something worth-while being patient and persistent for.

There is an old proverb which literally translated means, "By the servant the master is known." It is a good proverb for both the servant and the mistress to remember.

CHAPTER II

DINNERS

ABOUT THE AMERICAN HOSTESS

The greatest pride of the American hostess is her formal dinner. And it is to her credit that we mention that she can hold her own against the most aristocratic families of Europe.

There is a story told of a well-known New York society matron who gave a formal dinner party on every occasion that warranted it, no matter how trivial, for the reason that it gave her keen pleasure and enjoyment to do so. At one of her dinners recently a famous world-touring lecturer was the guest of honor—and the hostess was as happy and proud as it is possible for a hostess to be. Especially was she proud of the delectable menu she had ordered prepared for the occasion.

But much to her chagrin, she noticed that her distinguished guest was not eating the tempting hot dishes—only the vegetables, and relishes and fruits. She did not wish to appear rude, but she could not wait until dinner was over before asking him why he was not eating. "I am a vegetarian," he answered, "and I never indulge in meats."

The hostess-of-many-dinners had an inspiration. Here was an opportunity to give a unique dinner—and nothing could be more delightful for her. A week later, she sent

23

24 BOOK OF ETIQUETTE

out invitations to all her friends requesting their presence at another formal dinner to be held in honor of the visiting lecturer. This time it was a vegetarian dinner. Suffice to say that it was a huge success.

Such is the hospitality of our American hostesses that they will concede to every whim and desire of their guests. They must be pleased at all costs. The dinner is not a success unless each guest leaves a little happier than when he came—and incidentally a little better pleased with the person who happens to be giving the dinner.

PLANNING THE FORMAL DINNER

First in importance, of course, is when shall the formal dinner be held? Any evening of the week may be selected —although Sunday is rarely chosen. The hour is usually between seven and eight o'clock. Invitations should be mailed a week or ten days before the date set for the dinner. The hostess may use her own judgment in deciding whether the invitations should be engraved on cards, or hand-written on note paper. The former is preferred for an elaborate dinner, the latter for a small one.

It must be remembered in inviting guests to dinner, that it is a breach of etiquette to invite a wife without her husband, or the opposite. A married couple must always be invited together. If there are other members of the family who are desired as guests at the dinner, separate invitations must be sent to them. A dinner card is always addressed to a husband and wife, and individually to single persons.

For the convenience of the host, it is a point of courtesy for every recipient of an invitation to dinner, to answer

DINNERS

promptly. A good rule is to decide immediately upon receiving it whether or not you will be able to attend, and follow it with a cordial answer within the next twenty-four hours. If you find that you must refuse, there must be a very good reason for doing so.

In planning the dinner party, the hostess must go over her list of friends and carefully select six or eight who would naturally be most congenial together. The number may even be as low as four, and while there can be no absolute limit to the number one may invite, there must never be more than the hostess can handle easily. If the guests are chosen carefully, with a regard for their likes and dislikes, the dinner is bound to be a happy one.

ARRANGING THE TABLE

To set the formal dinner table correctly is an art in itself.

The appointments of the modern dinner table are a delight. Services are of silver and china is of the finest. Both the square or round table are appropriate, the latter being the most popular since it is easier to make attractive. A mat of asbestos or a thickness of canton flannel is first spread on the table. Over this comes the snowy, linen table-cover, falling gracefully over the sides with the four points almost touching the floor. A place is laid for each guest. The most fashionable method is to have a large lace or embroidered doily in the center of the table, and smaller ones indicating the position of the guests. A centerpiece of glass, china, silver, is usually used, over the doily or without it, and on top of this flowers. Delicate ferns are sometimes used instead of flowers, although

BOOK OF ETIQUETTE

roses (hot-house roses when no others are obtainable) are always the favorite at an elaborate dinner.

STARTING AT THE CENTER

When the center ornament has been adjusted, it may be used as a mathematical base for all the rest of the table appointments. Candlesticks, either of silver or bronze, are artistic when placed at equal distance around the flowers. They diffuse a soft light upon the table, and by being an incentive to the recalling of old memories, they invoke conversation when there is danger of its lagging. It is one of the charms of candlelight—this power to bring up pleasant reminiscences. Between these stately guardians of the floral centerpiece may be placed small dishes containing preserved ginger, macaroons or bon-bons.

Salt-cellars and pepper-boxes are next located on the table, and the places are laid for the guests. The proper number of forks is placed to the left. The knives and spoons are placed at the right. They are placed in the order in which they are to be used. Not more than three forks should ever appear on the table at one time. If others are needed they should be placed with their respective courses. A small square of bread, or a roll, is in the center, covered with the folded napkin, and a little to the left are the several glasses.

Care must be taken in arranging the dinner table to have both sides balanced. There is an old maxim that says, "There must be a use for everything" and this holds especially true of the table of good taste. It must not be littered with useless articles, no matter how artistic or odd, for they hamper the movements of the guests and make things unnecessarily crowded. Butter rarely appears on

DINNERS

the table at the formal dinner; and condiments are brought in by the servant only as they are needed.

SOME IMPORTANT DETAILS

Menu-cards are no longer used at the formal dinner, unless it is in celebration of some auspicious occasion and honored guests are present. In this case, the hostess has the menus printed or engraved in a delicate script and has one placed beside the plate of each guest. A favorite fashion is to have them printed in French. Sometime one of these cards serves for two guests, although the hostess who takes a pride in her dinners will provide each guest with one, as it serves as an appropriate souvenir of the occasion.

The lighting effect of the dining-room is important. Instead of the candles on the table there may be an electric cluster high above the table, or small candle-power electric lights on the walls. These latter produce a soft effect which is most pleasing. Glaring lights of any kind should be avoided. Candles and electric lights should never be used in conjunction.

There is nothing more conducive to thorough enjoyment of an evening, to the thorough enjoyment of a menu, than when table and appointments are perfect and artistically simple. The hostess should give as much time and thought to the preparation and arrangement of the table, as she does to the planning of the menu. She will find that her guests will appreciate novel lighting effects, surprising color tones, unusual serving innovations. And she will find that a correctly laid table will add surprisingly to the entire success of her dinner party.

BOOK OF ETIQUETTE

TABLE ETIQUETTE

The importance of correct table etiquette cannot be over-emphasized. Nothing is more vulgar, than clumsy, awkward movements at the table, and it is certainly a sign of ill-breeding deliberately to fail to act in accordance with the rules of table etiquette. The rules of dinner etiquette should be studied carefully and just as carefully followed, if one wishes to be—and everyone does—a lady or a gentleman.

Perhaps the most important thing is one's bearing at table. Very often you see a seemingly cultured gentleman in a hotel dining-room or restaurant playing with the table silver or absent-mindedly clinking glasses together. This may be overlooked in the restaurant, but at a formal dinner it is essentially bad form. When the hands are not being used, they should rest quietly in the lap—never should the elbows be rested on the table. The chair should be neither too near nor too far from the table; both are ungraceful and awkward.

TABLE SERVICE

The dinner napkin is from twenty to twenty-four inches across. It is folded square unless the table is somewhat crowded, when it may be folded diagonally (after having been folded square) so as to give more space around the board. If the napkins are monogrammed the monogram should be placed so as to be in plain view.

At a formal dinner the first course is on the table when the guests enter the dining-room. It consists of oysters, a canape, a fruit cocktail, grapefruit or something else of

DINNERS 29

the same kind. Oysters on the half-shell are served bedded in crushed ice in a soup plate. This is placed on the service plate. A cocktail is served in a cocktail glass which is placed on a doily-covered plate which in turn is placed on the service plate. The silver for the first course may be on the table beside the soup spoon or it may be served with the course.

The waiter removes the first course entirely before the soup is placed. He stands at the left of each guest and removes the plates with his left hand. The soup in soup plates (not in a tureen) is placed on the service plates and when this course is over service plates as well as soup plates are removed and the entrée is served. If the plates for it are empty they are placed with the right hand but if the entrée is already on them they are placed with the left. If empty plates are supplied the waiter passes the entrée on a platter held on a folded napkin on his left hand, using his right hand to help balance it. Each guest serves himself.

At the conclusion of this course the plates are removed and empty warm plates placed for the meat course. The meat should be carved before it is brought to the table and after the waiter has served each person he serves the vegetables. If there is only one waiter it is more convenient to have the vegetables placed on the table in large vegetable dishes from which each guest serves himself. After the vegetables have gone around once they are removed but they may be passed once or twice again before the conclusion of the meal.

The salad follows. It may be served on each plate (and this is surely the more artistic way) or it may be served from a platter. After the salad the table is cleared of all plates that have been in use, of salt and pepper shakers or

BOOK OF ETIQUETTE

cellars and is crumbed before the dessert is brought in.

Usually the dessert which is nearly always ice-cream or something else frozen is served in individual dishes. Small cakes are passed with it. Other desserts besides ice-cream are served in much the same way.

When the dessert has been removed, finger-bowls half filled with water and placed on a small doily-covered plate are set before each person.

Coffee may be served at the table but it is more often served in the drawing-room.

USE OF THE NAPKIN

What can be more unsightly than a napkin tucked carefully in the top of one's waistcoat? And still, how often one sees it done among men who believe that they are impressively well-bred! The proper way to use a napkin, whether it is at a formal dinner, or in a restaurant, is to unfold it only half, leaving the center fold as it is. and lay it across the knees. It may be used constantly during the meal, whenever the guest finds need for it, but it must never be completely unfolded.

When rising from the table, the napkin is placed *as it is* on the table. It is never folded again into its original form, as that would be an assumption on the part of the guest that the hostess would use it again before laundering. A reprehensible habit is to drop the napkin carelessly into the finger-bowl, or over the coffee cup. It should be laid *on* the table, at the right of the finger-bowl.

THE SPOON AT THE DINNER TABLE

Spoons are used when eating grapefruit and other fruits served with cream. Jellies, puddings, custards,

DINNERS

porridges, preserves and boiled eggs are always eaten with spoons. Also, of course, soup, bouillon, coffee and tea. In the case of the three latter beverages, however, the spoon is used only to stir them once or twice and to taste them to see that they are of the desired temperature. It is never allowed to stand in the cup while the beverage is being drunk. Nor is it permissible to draw up a spoonful of soup or coffee and blow upon it; one must wait until it is sufficiently cooled of itself. In taking soup, the correct way to use the spoon is to dip it with an outward motion instead of drawing it towards one. The soup is then imbibed from the side, not the end.

THE FORK AND KNIFE

In using the fork and knife, one can display a pleasing grace, or just the opposite—awkward clumsiness. It depends entirely upon how well one knows and follows the correct rules. The first rule to be remembered is that a knife is never used for any other purpose than cutting food. It is unforgiveable to use a knife to convey food to the mouth—unforgiveable and vulgar. The knife is held in the right hand and the fork in the left. When the desired morsel of food is cut, the knife is laid aside temporarily and the fork is shifted to the right hand.

The knife and fork should never be held in the same hand together, and when not being used, one or both of the utensils should rest on the plate. They should never be allowed to rest against the edge of the plate with the handles on the table; when one is through with both the knife and fork, they should be placed entirely on the plate, their tips touching at the center, their handles resting

BOOK OF ETIQUETTE

against the edge. They are never placed back again on the table.

The foods eaten with the fork are meats, vegetables, fish, salads, oysters and clams, lobster, ices, frozen puddings and melons. Hearts of lettuce and lettuce leaves are folded up with the fork and conveyed uncut to the mouth. If the leaves are too large to be folded conveniently, they may be cut with the blunt edge of the fork—never with a knife.

FINGER FOODS

Various foods are eaten with the fingers instead of fork or spoon. Bread, for instance, is never cut but always broken into small pieces and lifted to the mouth with the fingers. Butter is seldom provided at the formal dinner, but if it is, each little piece of bread is buttered individually just before it is eaten. Crackers and cake are eaten in the same way; although some cakes and pastries are eaten with the fork. Those that can be eaten daintily with the fingers such as macaroons, lady-fingers, cookies, etc., should be eaten so while layer cake and elaborate pastries should be eaten with the fork.

Corn on the cob is without a doubt one of the most difficult foods to eat gracefully. And yet it is too delicious to forego the pleasure of eating it at all. It is entirely permissible to use the fingers in eating corn, holding it lightly at each end; sometimes a napkin is used in holding it. Many a foresighted hostess, when serving corn on the cob, provides each guest with a short, keen, steel-bladed knife with which the kernels may be cut from the cob easily. This is by far the most satisfactory method.

French artichokes are also difficult to eat. The proper

Photo by Bradley and Merrill. Courtesy of the *Pictoria Reve*

TABLE SET FOR DINNER

The decoration in the center of the table should never be so high as to form an obstruction

DINNERS

way is to break them apart, leaf by leaf, dip the tips in the sauce and lift them to the mouth with the fingers. The heart is cut and eaten with a fork.

Lobster claws may be pulled apart with the fingers. Shrimps also, when served whole in their shells, may be separated, peeled and eaten with the fingers. Fruits such as oranges, apples, grapes, peaches and plums are all eaten with the fingers. Celery, radishes and olives are similarly eaten. Sometimes there are other relishes on the dinner table, and the guest must use his common sense to determine whether they are eaten with the fork or fingers. Bonbons, of course, are always eaten with the fingers.

Whenever fruits are served the finger-bowl should follow. It is always used at the completion of the dinner. The bowl is half filled with tepid water and set upon a plate. A fragrant leaf may be added to the water. The fingers are dipped lightly into the bowl, one hand at a time, and then dried on the napkin. It is a mark of ill-breeding to splash the water about, to put both hands into the bowl at once, or to wet the entire palm of the hand. Only the finger tips should touch the water.

TABLE ACCIDENTS

"Accidents will happen"—at the dinner table as well as anywhere else. The duty of the guest and the hostess both is to see that no confusion and embarrassment follows.

If a spoon or fork or napkin is dropped, the proper thing to do is to allow the servant to pick it up; the well-trained servant will not return it, but place it aside and give the guest another one. If a glass or cup is dropped

BOOK OF ETIQUETTE

and broken, embarrassed apologies will not put it together again, but a word of sincere regret to the hostess will relieve the awkwardness of the moment, and will be as gratifying to her as profuse apologies. If the article broken is a valuable one, the guest may replace it by sending, a day or two later, another one as nearly like it as possible. A cordial note of regret may accompany it.

Sometimes a cup of coffee or a glass of water is overturned at the table. This is, of course, a very serious and unpleasant accident, but there is no necessity in making matters worse by fussing about it and offering several exaggerated apologies. A simple word or two to the hostess will suffice; but it is really quite important that one should be careful not to let an accident of this kind happen too often, otherwise one will soon acquire the reputation of being a clumsy boor.

There is certainly no reason to feel embarrassed when an accident occurs at the dinner table—that is, of course, if it was not due to carelessness. It is not the accident itself that will cause the guests and the hostess to consider one ill-bred, but continued mention of it and many flustered apologies. "I am sorry" or "How careless of me!" are sufficient offers of regret—the matter should then be forgotten.

THE HOSTESS

Important indeed are the duties of the hostess, for it is upon her that the ultimate success of the dinner depends. It is not enough to send out the invitations, plan a delectable menu and supervise the laying of the table. She must afford pleasant diversion and entertainment for her guests from the minute they enter her home until

DINNERS

they are ready to leave. The ideal hostess is the one who can make her guests, one and all, feel better satisfied with themselves and the world in general when they leave her home than they did when they arrived.

WHEN THE GUESTS ARRIVE

The duty of receiving and welcoming the guests rests with the host and hostess. They receive in the drawing-room until fifteen or twenty minutes after the time mentioned in the invitations. Then, even if there is still a guest or two missing, it is customary for dinner to be served. Only on one occasion does this rule vary; if the dinner is being held in honor of some celebrated guest, it may not be served until he has arrived.

The hostess, in inviting her guests, should be sure that there is an equal number of men and women. Husbands and wives should never be sent into the dining-room together. The usual order of precedence is as follows: The host leads with the lady who is to sit at his right; if the dinner is in honor of a married couple, the host goes in to dinner with the wife of the honored guest; the hostess ending the "procession" with that lady's husband. When there are no guests of honor the host takes the eldest lady present. Usually a lady visiting the house for the first time is the first to enter the dining-room. If there is one more woman than men in the party, the customary thing is for the hostess to enter the dining-room alone after all her guests have entered it. She must never take the other arm of the last gentleman.

The seating should be arranged by placing cards bearing the names of each guest next to each plate if the party is a large one. This method may be pursued if the party

BOOK OF ETIQUETTE

is small, though, in this case it is quite possible for the hostess to indicate gracefully the place where she wishes each guest to sit. The guests who enter the dining-room together sit side by side; the hostess always waits until everyone is seated, before she takes her place and motions that the dinner is to proceed.

When a guest arrives late, the hostess must endeavor to make him feel at ease and unembarrassed. If the guest is a woman, she rises, greets her cordially and conducts her to her place without mentioning her lateness. If it is a man, she merely bows and smiles without rising and immediately starts a lively discussion or interesting conversation to draw attention away from the late arrival. In this manner he is put at ease, and the incident is promptly forgotten.

THE SUCCESSFUL HOSTESS

The hostess must see that all her guests are comfortable and well taken care of. She must stimulate conversation and help things along by herself relating amusing little anecdotes or experiences. She must not introduce any topic, however, that would in the least detail suggest scandal or gossip.

Nothing is more delightful, at the dinner table, whether formal or informal, than the interesting little chats between old friends and new acquaintances. Special musical programs always please dinner guests, and when held after dinner are usually appreciated. In selecting musical numbers the hostess should bear in mind the personal likes and dislikes of her guests. Music during the meal if

DINNERS

it is soft enough not to interfere with conversation is pleasing, though it is not essential. The musicians should be hidden behind palms.

Happy is she, who, at the conclusion of the formal dinner, can say to herself that everything was as it should be; that each of the guests had an enjoyable time; that the entire dinner had been a success. And she may claim the success of the evening as her own, for it is upon the hostess that each phase of successful dinner-giving devolves, even when most of the actual entertaining is done by one or more of the guests.

THE GUEST

When Gung-Yee-Far-Choy (the Chinese two-week New Year) comes, our yellow cousins make their formal visits. It is a time of extreme convention, and despite the seeming revelry and celebration, the strictest rules are observed. The calls are made according to the callers' rank. One pays visits to those superior, receiving in turn those inferior. It is perplexing to know just how they decide which is superior and which inferior in each case. Perhaps it is their Oriental instinct.

But the American guest does not have to determine whether he is superior to his host and hostess—or the opposite. It is already decided for him, by the laws of etiquette. For the guest at the formal dinner must accord every respect and honor to his host and hostess— not in the servile manner of the coolie towards the mandarin, of course—but in the captivating and charming manner that bespeaks the fine lady and gentleman.

BOOK OF ETIQUETTE

COMMENTS ON FOOD

Men and women of cultivation rarely make comments on food except to praise. It is better to accept a little of each course on one's place and eat a bit of it although one does not particularly care for it, than to refuse it entirely. A highly amusing story is related of a guest who was invited to a formal dinner given by a prominent New York woman who had gained a reputation for the savory qualities of the soups she served. On this occasion she was especially proud of her Grun Yung Waa (Bird's-Nest Soup)—and really, from all reports, it must have been remarkably delicious. But the guest we are writing about, sniffed at the soup disdainfully and asked, "Is this some of that new canned soup they are advertising?" The hostess blushed—as any conscientious hostess would—and the next time she issued invitations for dinner, she somehow forgot to include the guest who read the advertisements so diligently.

SECOND HELPINGS

A guest at a formal dinner should never ask for a second helping of any dish. This holds equally true for an elaborate luncheon. However, the host or hostess may offer to provide a second helping to any one of the guests who has disposed of his first helping. In this case, the guest may acknowledge it with a smile, or if his appetite is entirely satisfied, he may refuse it with a polite word of thanks.

To insist, on the part of the host, after the guest has refused a second helping, is overdoing the bounds of hos-

DINNERS

pitality, and perilously borders on the verge of inci-
vility.

THE MENU

The hostess must be careful not to apologize profusely
for things which are not as she would like to have them;
it is better form completely to ignore the fact that the
salad is not crisp enough or that the entrée is too highly
seasoned. The entire time spent at table should be no
more than an hour and a half. An hour is usually sufficient if the courses are served with expedition. But
there must be no semblance of haste.

Good cook books are full of suggestions for delectable
menus and for the order of service. The butler or maid
takes complete charge and it is better to have a less elaborate dinner than to have so many courses that he or she
cannot manage without haste, noise, or confusion. The
order of service depends upon the number of courses.
The cook book will help here, also. Generally speaking,
oysters on the half shell buried in ice, a cocktail, or a fruit
cup constitutes the first course. This is followed by soup,
game or fish, a salad, the roast and vegetables, dessert
and coffee.

In presenting the first course the lady at the right of
the host is served first. After that the order is varied
so that the same person will not be served last every time.
The butler serves dishes from the left and removes them
from the right. No plates for any course are removed
until everyone has finished. It is not necessary to wait
until everyone is served to begin eating but it is most
vulgar to show undue haste.

It is the duty of the butler to keep the glasses filled

BOOK OF ETIQUETTE

with water and to see that nuts, bonbons, etc., are passed frequently.

When fruit is served, the butler places a glass dessert-plate on which is an embroidered doily and finger-bowl, before each guest, and next to it a small fruit knife. Then the fruits are offered to each guest; and when the hostess is quite sure that everyone has finished, she makes the sign for retiring. The usual manner of doing this, is to catch the eye of the lady who is the partner of her husband for the evening, nod and smile to her, and they both rise together, followed immediately by the other women guests. They adjourn to the drawing-room, where coffee is served and light conversation ensues until the men join them. The latter, in the meanwhile, remain in the dining-room to smoke their cigars and drink their coffee. Usually they will leave their original seats and move up to the end of the table, gathering around the host, whose duty it now is to entertain them and to keep pleasant conversation going. Fifteen minutes is an ample time for the gentlemen to smoke and chat by themselves. Then they are expected to join the ladies in the drawing-room.

SPECIAL ENTERTAINMENT

Some hostesses like to provide special entertainment for their guests—professional dancers, elocutionists, or singers. But here "circumstances must alter cases." As a matter of fact, not very much entertainment is really required, for if the guests are congenial, they will no doubt enjoy conversation among themselves. It is, of course, not necessary to limit one's conversation to the lady or gentleman with whom one's lot has been cast for the eve-

DINNERS

41

ning. However, special attention should be paid to that person,

WHEN TO LEAVE

It is only an extremely rude and discourteous guest who will leave immediately upon the conclusion of the dinner. The correct thing to do, when invited to a dinner that begins at eight o'clock is to order one's car to appear at the door at ten-thirty. In most cases, however, when the guests are brilliant and pleasant, and when conversation holds one in spite of the desire to leave, it is customary to remain until eleven o'clock when the party will, no doubt, break up entirely.

In these days of gay festivities and continual hospitalities, it is not unusual for a popular guest to be invited to two receptions in one evening. Even this urgent responsibility, however, does not warrant the guest's hurrying away while the dinner is still serving—though it may be the last stages. The courteous way is to wait until all the guests have adjourned to the drawing-room, remain fifteen or twenty minutes conversing with one's partner or other guests, and then with a fitting apology and brief explanation, order one's car. If this is followed, the hostess cannot feel any dissatisfaction or resentment; but the guest who insists on rushing away, shows ill-breeding and inconsideration.

TAKING LEAVE

The lady, whether she be wife, sister or fiancée, is the first to express a desire to depart. When she does, she and the gentleman will seek out the host and hostess, thank them cordially for their hospitality, and take their leave.

42   BOOK OF ETIQUETTE

Here are some accepted forms that may be used with variations according to the guest's own personality:

"Good-night, Mrs. Carr.   I must thank you for
a perfectly delightful evening."

To which the hostess will no doubt answer something to this effect:

"We were glad to have you, I'm sure, Mrs. Roberts."

Here is another manner in which to extend one's thanks, and how to accept them:

"Sorry we must start so soon, Mrs. Carr.
Thank you so much for your kindness."
"Good-night, Mrs. Roberts.   I hope to see you
soon again."

It is also very important to bid one's partner for the evening a cordial good-night.   In fact, it is a flagrant breach to leave without having thanked one's partner— and a gentleman will never do it.   A word or two is all that is necessary.

The hostess, in taking leave of her guests, will gratefully acknowledge their thanks and say a word or two expressing her pleasure at their presence.   It is not civil or courteous on the part of either host or hostess to attempt to prolong the presence of any guest after he has made it known that he wishes to depart.

INVITING A STOP-GAP

If the hostess finds, almost at the last moment, that one of her guests is unavoidably detained and will not be

DINNERS 43

able to attend the dinner, she may call upon a friend to take the vacant place. The friend thus invited should not feel that he or she is playing "second-fiddle" and the fact that she was not invited at first should not tempt her to refuse the invitation which would be a serious discourtesy, indeed. Quite on the contrary, she should accept cordially, and then do her utmost to make her (or his, as the case may be) presence at the dinner amiable and pleasant.

The invitation is usually in the form of a hand-written note, explaining the reason for its last-minute arrival, and frankly requesting the presence of the lady or gentleman in the place of the one who cannot appear. The answer should be brief but sincere; there must be no hint in it that the recipient is not altogether pleased with the invitation and with the idea of dining in someone's else place. To refuse an invitation to serve as a stop-gap, without an acceptable reason for doing so is an inexcusable violation of the rules of good breeding.

Of course, it is not always agreeable to the hostess to call on one of her friends to attend her dinner in the place of someone else; but it is certainly a better plan than to leave the guest out entirely, and have one more lady than gentleman, or *vice versa*. If the note is cordial and frankly sincere, a good friend will not feel any unreasonable resentment, but will, in fact, be pleased to serve.

SIMPLE DINNERS

The simple dinner, perfectly achieved, is as admirable a feat as the elaborate dinner, perfectly achieved. The hostess who has attained the art of giving perfect din-

44 BOOK OF ETIQUETTE

ners, though they are small, may well be proud of her attainment.

If the cook knows how to cook; if the maid is well-trained, and correctly attired in white cap and apron and black dress; if the table is laid according to the rules of dinner etiquette; if the welcome is cordial and the company congenial—the simple dinner may rank with the most extravagant and elaborate formal dinner. The cover may contain fewer pieces and the menu may contain fewer courses, the setting may be less fashionable, though not less harmonious, and still the dinner may be extremely tempting and enjoyable.

INVITING CONGENIAL GUESTS

Perhaps it is more important to select the guests wisely at a small informal dinner than it is at a formal one. As there are usually only four or six guests, they will undoubtedly become well acquainted by the time the dinner is over, and in order to have agreeable conversation it is necessary that they be congenial.

In a week or two, one generally forgets just what food was eaten at a certain dinner—but if the guests were all amiable and pleasing, the memory of conversation with them will linger and be constantly associated with the hostess and her home. Many a hostess would be happier (and her guests, too) if less time were paid to the planning of a menu, and more time spent in choosing guests who will be happy together.

WHEN THERE ARE NO SERVANTS

There is no reason why lack of servants should prevent one from entertaining friends and extending one's

DINNERS 45

hospitality. The ideal hostess is not the one who tries to outdo her neighbor—who attempts, even though it is beyond her means, to give elaborate dinners that vie favorably with those given by her neighbors. The simplest dinner has possibilities of being a huge success, if it is given in the spirit of true cordiality.

For instance, a dinner which the writer attended recently was given by a young woman who did not have any servants. There were six guests who all had mutual interests and with very little help from the hostess they were not long in finding them.

The table was laid for eight. A silver bowl containing delicate ferns graced the center. The lights were shaded to a soft radiance. The entire dining-room had an atmosphere of quiet and restfulness about it. Each guest found, upon taking his place for dinner, a tall fruit glass at his cover, containing crushed grapefruit and cherries. When this first course was finished, the hostess placed the glasses on a serving table and wheeled it into the kitchen. The kitchen adjoined the dining-room, which of course facilitated matters considerably. And yet it was sufficiently separated to exclude all unpleasant signs of cooking.

There was no confusion, no haste, no awkward pauses. Somehow, the guests seemed to forget that maids or butlers were necessary at all. The quiet, calm poise of the hostess dominated the entire party and everyone felt contented and at ease.

There was a complete absence of restraint of any kind; conversation flowed smoothly and naturally, and in the enjoyment of one another's company, the guests were as happy and satisfied as they would probably have been at an elaborate formal dinner.

BOOK OF ETIQUETTE

A table service wagon is most useful for the woman who is her own maid. It stands at the right of the hostess and may be wheeled in and out as she finds it necessary, though for the in ormal dinner it should not be essential to move it once it is in place. In the drawer should be found one or two extra napkins and extra silver for each course in case of accident or emergency. The coffee service may be placed on top of the table with the dishes for the several courses arranged on the shelves of the table from top to bottom in the order in which they are to be used. The table should not be too heavily loaded. It is much more useful when things are "easy to get at."

If your home is small and inconvenient, if you become easily flustered, if you don't find intense pleasure in mak· ing others happy, then don't invite friends to dinner— and discomfort. But if you are the jolly, calm, happy sort of a hostess, who can attend to duties quickly and yet without confusion, if you have a cozy little home and taste enough to make it attractive—then give dinners by all means,—and your guests will not object to their simplicity.

HOTEL DINNERS

With the servant problem growing more complex every year, more and more hostesses are turning to hotels to provide their special dinners. These cannot rival a successful dinner at home but often they are much easier to arrange and even the most conservative of hostesses may entertain dinner guests at a hotel. Private dining-rooms are a luxury but much more charming than the public room. The latter is, of course, the one used by the large majority of people.

DINNERS 47

Most hotels provide comfortable lobbies or lounges in which guests may wait for each other. But if the hotel is a big one and crowded it is pleasanter to meet elsewhere and arrive together.

The etiquette of the hotel dining-room is that of the home dining-room. Nothing should ever be done to draw attention to the group of people who are dining there. Quiet behavior is more than ever valuable.

DRESS FOR DINNER

For an informal dinner a woman may wear a semi-evening dress of the sort suitable for afternoon while her partner wears the regular dinner jacket. For a formal affair formal *décolleté* dress with the hair arranged somewhat more elaborately than usual is required. Jewels may be worn. Gloves are always removed, never at a dinner should they be tucked in at the wrists. Men, of course, wear full evening dress to a formal dinner.

In hotels and other public dining-rooms there is more freedom of choice as to what one shall wear but it is in bad taste to attitre oneself conspicuously. A woman dining alone should always wear her hat into the dining-room even if she is a guest of the hotel.

It is amazing how much the little niceties of life have to do with making a dinner pleasant, and in every home the family should "dress for dinner" even though this may not mean donning regulation evening dress. Formal or informal, in the intimacy of the family circle or in a large group of friends the meal should be unhurried and calm.

CHAPTER III

LUNCHEONS

PURPOSE OF THE LUNCHEON

In England, and especially in London, the luncheon is held in quite as high esteem as our most formal dinners. For it is at the luncheon, in England, that distinguished men and women meet to discuss the important topics of the moment and exchange opinions. It is indeed easy to understand why this would be a delightful meal, for there is none of the restraint and formality of the late dinner.

But in America, perhaps because most all of our gentlemen are at business "down-town" during the day, perhaps because we disdain to ape England's customs, the luncheon has not yet reached the point where it rivals the formal dinner. And yet it holds rather an important place all its own.

The "place" is distinctly feminine. The ladies of America have taken the luncheon in hand and developed it into a splendid midday entertainment and means of hospitality. The gentlemen are of course welcome; but they are rarely present. It is usually among themselves that the ladies celebrate the ceremony of the luncheon—both formal and informal—and that it has survived, and is tending to become permanently popular, is sufficient proof of its success. It is often preceded or followed by cards or other simple entertainment.

LUNCHEONS 49

INFORMAL LUNCHEONS

Invitations may be sent only a few days before the day set for the luncheon, and are usually written in the first person instead of the third which is the convention for more elaborate functions. The hour of luncheon is stated, but need not be as rigidly followed as the dinner hour. If guests are reasonably late they may be excused, but the late dinner guest is correctly considered discourteous. Lord Houghton, famous in England's social history, used to word his invitations simply "Come and lunch with me to-morrow" or "Will you lunch with me Tuesday?" He rarely mentioned the hour. Incidentally, Lord Houghton's unceremonious luncheons earned for him widespread comment, and they had much to do with the ultimate popularity of the informal luncheon in England.

The informal luncheon lost none of its easy congeniality in traveling across the ocean. There is a certain friendliness that distinguishes this meal from all others. Sometimes, in fact, the hostess dispenses with the ceremony of service altogether, and her guests help themselves from the buffet or side-table. If such is the case, the luncheon consists of cold meats, ham, tongue, roast beef, etc.; salads, wine jellies, fruits, cakes, bonbons and coffee. The most usual way, however, is to serve a more substantial luncheon, retaining just that degree of dinner formality that is so gratifying to the social sense.

ABOUT THE TABLE

Often the informal luncheon is served on the bare table, making use of numerous lace or linen doilies instead of

50 BOOK OF ETIQUETTE

the usual table-cloth. (This does not hold true of the formal luncheon and may not be true even of the informal one.)

The menu must be appropriate to the season. Tea or coffee are never served in the drawing-room after the informal luncheon. If at all, they are served right at the table at the conclusion of the meal.

The informal luncheon guest never remains long after the luncheon unless the hostess has provided special amusement. If the luncheon lasts an hour the guests may sit around and chat with the hostess for about a half hour; but they must remember that she may have afternoon engagements, and it would be exceedingly inconsiderate and rude on their part to delay her.

THE FORMAL LUNCHEON

The formal luncheon is very much like the formal dinner, except that it is not so substantial as to menu. The table is laid the same, except that linen doilies are used in preference to table-cloths. The latter are in good form, however, and it is merely a matter of taste in the final selection. Then too, there is never any artificial light at a luncheon, whether it be simple or elaborate.

The formal luncheon usually opens with a first course of fruit—grapefruit, ordinarily, but sometimes chilled pineapple or fruit cocktails. When the fruit glasses are removed, bouillon in two-handled cups is served. Sometimes a course of fish follows, but it is really not essential to the luncheon and most hostesses prefer to omit it. An entrée is next served—chicken, mushrooms, sweetbreads or beef according to the taste and judgment of the hostess; and usually a vegetable accompanies it.

LUNCHEONS

A light salad, prepared with a regard for harmony with the rest of the menu, is always acceptable at the luncheon. Desserts may be the same as those served for dinner,— jellies, frozen puddings, ice-cream, tarts, nuts, etc. It is not customary to retire to the drawing-room for coffee; it is good form to have it served at the table. If the weather is tempting, and if the hostess is so inclined, coffee may be served on the porch. However, these lesser details must be decided by personal taste and convenience.

It may be taken for granted that the hostess would not give a formal luncheon if she had afternoon engagements. For that reason, the guests may stay later than they would at an informal luncheon. Sometimes music is provided, and often there are recitations and dramatic readings. Usually the hour set for a ceremonious luncheon is one-thirty o'clock; it is safe to say, then, that three o'clock or half-past three is ample time to take one's departure.

THE TABLE FOR THE FORMAL LUNCHEON

The appointments of the formal luncheon table are, as was pointed out above, almost identical with those of the dinner table.

In the first place, butter may be served with the formal luncheon and rarely with dinner. Thus we find tiny butter dishes added at the left of each luncheon cover. These plates are usually decorative, and sometimes are made large enough to contain both the bread and butter, instead of just the butter alone. Another difference, though slight:—cut-glass platters for nuts and bonbons take the place of the silver platters of dinner. Candles are not used; nor is any other artificial light whenever it can be avoided.

BOOK OF ETIQUETTE

The formal luncheon offers an ideal time for the hostess to display her finest china, her best silver. It is an occasion when dignity and beauty combine with easy friendliness to make the event memorable, and the wise hostess spares no effort in adding those little touches that go so far towards making any entertainment a success. Menu cards and favors, of course, are "touches" that belong to the dinner table alone; but flowers, service and general setting of the dining-room are details that deserve considerable attention and thought.

HOSTESS AND GUEST

The primary requisite of a successful luncheon is harmonious and agreeable relationship between hostess and guests. This holds true both of the formal and informal luncheons, though particularly of the former. One cannot possibly enjoy a luncheon—no matter how carefully the menu has been prepared, no matter how delightful the environment—if there are awkward lapses in the conversation; if there are moments of painful, embarrassing silence; or if the conversation is stilted, affected or forced.

Spontaneity of conversation and ease of manner, together with a hostess who knows how to plan delightful little surprises, and simple though delicious menus,— these are the secrets of successful luncheon-giving. And if they cannot be observed, the hostess had better direct her energies toward strictly formal entertainments; the luncheon is not one of her accomplishments.

The hostess receives in her drawing-room. She rises as each guest enters the room, greets her, or him, as the case may be, with outstretched hand, and proceeds with any necessary introductions. As soon as all the guests

LUNCHEONS

have arrived, she orders luncheon served, and she herself leads the way to the dining-room. The guests may seat themselves in the manner that is most congenial; but in arranging the formal luncheon, the hostess usually identifies the correct seat with a small place card. If there is a guest of honor, or a lady whom the hostess wishes to show deference to, she is given the place to the right of the hostess.

If there are gentlemen at the formal luncheon, including the hostess' husband, they do not remain at the table to smoke and chat as they do after dinner, but leave the dining-room with the ladies. Neither do they offer the ladies their arms when entering or leaving the dining-room. If the host is considerate, and is fortunate enough to have a porch, she will suggest that the gentlemen have their cigars on the porch.

A well-bred guest will never take advantage of the leniency toward late-comers to the luncheon. It is *always* rude to keep people waiting; but it is doubly so to be lax in one's punctuality because one rule is not as exacting as another. The guest must also bear in mind that a great part of the enjoyment of the luncheon devolves upon his or her own cordiality and friendliness. Every guest must feel it a duty to supply some of the conversation, and if he is not naturally conversant, it might be wise to decide upon and remember several interesting little anecdotes that the company will enjoy hearing. No one can be excused from silence or lack of interest at the luncheon.

To the hostess, then, goes the responsibility of providing the means of enjoyment; to the guests goes the responsibility of utilizing this means, and coöperating with the hostess in making the entire thing a success. There

BOOK OF ETIQUETTE

are huge social possibilities in the luncheon, and it is rapidly becoming one of America's favorite functions. With both hostess and guest observing their duties, it must inevitably be a triumph that will vie with the important dignity of the formal dinner itself.

FORMAL AND INFORMAL BREAKFASTS

Breakfast to some people may mean a hastily swallowed cup of tea or coffee, and a bit of roll or cake. The early breakfast, of course. But to many there is a later breakfast that is as elaborate as it is tempting.

The formal breakfast may be held any time between ten and twelve-thirty. A fruit course opens the menu, with a mild *hors d'œuvre* following. Soup is never served. After the fruit, fish, broiled or *sauté* is served, and sometimes deviled lobster if it is preferred. In England, steamed finnan haddie is the favorite breakfast fish.

The personal tastes of the guests must be taken into consideration in deciding upon the main course. Lamb or veal chops are acceptable, and egg dishes are always welcomed. They may be accompanied by mushrooms, small French peas or potatoes. For the next course, chicken meets with favor especially if it is broiled or fried with rice. Dessert of frozen punch, pastry or jellies follows immediately after the chicken; and coffee, in breakfast cups, concludes the meal. And of course, the hot muffins and crisp biscuits of breakfast fame are not forgotten—nor the waffles and syrup, either, if one is partial to them.

For an informal breakfast, the menu is correspondingly less elaborate. Once again it begins with fruit, and it may be followed by the good old-fashioned course of

LUNCHEONS

ham or bacon and eggs with johnny-cake and potatoes; or the simple breakfast may be started with cereal, served with cream, and followed with broiled finnan haddie and baked potatoes. Eggs, quail or chops, and a crisp salad is another menu often adapted to the late informal breakfast. Desserts should be simple; sweets are seldom indulged in at breakfast. Buns with marmalade or honey are always acceptable, and frozen puddings seem to be a just-right finish to a delicious breakfast.

The informal breakfast is given at ten or eleven o'clock in the morning. It is never very elaborate; it is, in fact, one of the simplest, yet most dignified of informal meals.

DRESS FOR LUNCHEONS AND BREAKFASTS

Whether she is hostess or guest the woman at a breakfast or luncheon should wear an afternoon gown of silk, *crêpe-de-chine*, velvet, cloth or novelty material. In the summer preference may be given organdies, georgettes, etc. The simpler the affair the simpler the costume should be.

Men may wear the cutaway coat if the luncheon is a formal one while for simpler affairs the sack coat or summer flannels, when the season is appropriate, may be worn.

CHAPTER IV

TEAS AND OTHER ENTERTAINMENTS

EVOLUTION OF THE AFTERNOON TEA

Of course one cannot mention the words "afternoon tea" without immediately associating it with merry England. For it was there that, over two hundred years ago, a dreamy-eyed Dutchman (dreamy-eyed because he had lived many years in China) brought with him from the Orient a peculiar little leaf which, with a little hot water and sugar, made a delicious drink. At first lordly Englishmen would have none of him—but he didn't care. He exhibited the powers of the little leaves, made his tea, and drank it with evident relish. Others were curious; they, too, drank, and once they started it was difficult to do without it.

Someone spread the rumor that this new drink from China contained drugs and stimulants—and no sooner was this rumor spread than everyone began drinking it! Even the ladies and gentlemen of better society finally condescended to taste "the stuff"—and lo! before they realized it, it had been unconsciously adopted as their very own beverage! Through two generations the idea of the afternoon tea has been perfected, until to-day we have cosy, delightful, ceremonious five-o'clock teas that are the pride of the English and the joy of everyone who follows the custom.

TEAS AND OTHER ENTERTAINMENTS 57

And so we find the afternoon tea enjoying a vogue of unrivaled popularity here in America. When a *débutante* daughter is to be introduced to society, the mother plans an elaborate afternoon tea (and they can certainly be elaborate!). When guests from out-of-town are visiting, the hostess can think of nothing more appropriate than a chummy tea to introduce them to her friends. So charming a way of entertaining is the afternoon tea that it has usurped the evening reception almost entirely, except when the occasion requires special formality.

THE SIMPLER TEA

Then, too, there is the simpler tea so dear to the hearts of our hospitable ladies of good society. It was George Eliot who earnestly inquired, "Reader, have you ever drunk a cup of tea?" There is something undeniably heart-warming and conversation-making in a cup of steaming hot tea served with delicious cream; it is an ideal prescription for banishing loneliness. Perhaps it is not so much the tea itself, as the circle of happy friends eager for a pleasant chat.

As the simple tea does not require very much preparation or planning, we will discuss it briefly here and take up only the formal tea in detail. The simple tea may be served for any guest who chances in between four or six o'clock in the afternoon. Sometimes a hostess devotes a stated time each day or on certain days in the week which are known to her friends, to tea, and she lets her friends know just what the hour is and that they are welcome to join for a bite and a little chat whenever they feel so inclined. There may be one or several little tea tables which are brought into the drawing-room when the

BOOK OF ETIQUETTE

guests are ready for tea. Covering each one is a dainty lace or linen doily, or an embroidered tea-cloth. If tea tables are not available, one large table may serve the purpose, but it also must be covered with small doilies at each cover instead of one large table-cloth.

The hostess and one or two of her friends may serve. The tea is made at the table and served with very small, dainty sandwiches and all kinds of quaintly-shaped cakes. Bonbons, salted nuts and sometimes ices are also served.

If the hostess does not own dainty tea equipage, the beverage may be made in the kitchen and brought in ready to serve, fragrant and steaming. The custom of the afternoon tea is confined almost wholly to women, though it is not bad form by any means to have gentlemen present for tea.

A tea wagon offers the most attractive service for an afternoon tea. It should not be in the room where the hostess receives but should be wheeled in from an adjoining room (the dining-room usually). The maid, if there is one, performs this service, the hostess herself if there is no maid. The table should not be overcrowded and if there is not ample room for sandwich trays these should be brought in separately.

The china should be thin and of the same general kind though not necessarily of the same pattern. There should be sugar—preferably block sugar with tongs, a pitcher of cream, slices of lemon, mint leaves and cloves. If the hostess makes the tea herself she adds sugar, cream, lemon or whatever else the guest may desire before she passes the cup. The hostess who cares about her reputation for hospitality will perfect herself in the gentle art of making delicious tea before the day comes for her to prove herself before her guests.

TEAS AND OTHER ENTERTAINMENTS   59

THE FORMAL TEA

When the afternoon tea becomes formal and ceremonious it takes the place of the customary "at home." Invitations must be sent a week or ten days in advance, and if one is unable to attend, a polite note of explanation must be sent. However, no answer is necessary if one intends to be present.

With this more pretentious affair, the refreshments are served in the dining-room instead of in the drawing-room or outdoors as is sometimes done at simpler teas. The hissing urn always holds the place of honor (except on very warm days when iced tea or iced coffee may be served). Trays of thinly sliced bread are on the table, and dainty sandwiches in large variety. Fruit salads are never amiss, and strawberries with cream are particularly delightful when in season. Then, of course, there are cakes and bonbons and ices, although the latter are usually confined to warm days.

At a ceremonious tea, the hostess stands near the drawing-room door to greet each guest as she arrives. If her daughters receive with her, they stand to her right, and help in making any necessary introductions. As many guests as can be conveniently entertained may be invited to the formal tea; but the refreshments must never be so substantial that they will interfere with dinner. In fact, the tea must be kept true to its name, for if other eatables besides those fashionable to the tea are served, it is a reception in substance if not in name.

When one wishes to invite eighteen or twenty friends, and does not wish to undertake the trouble or expense of a dinner, the "high tea" is in order. It is usually held

BOOK OF ETIQUETTE

on a Sunday evening. At these "high teas" small tables are invariably used, four guests being placed at each table. It is customary to allow the guests to form their own quartettes, for in this manner they will usually find table companions who will be congenial—and a most unfortunate occurrence at a "high tea," or in fact any reception, is a seating arrangement untasteful to the guests themselves. The little tables are covered with snowy tea cloths and decorated with a sprig of flowers in a colored vase occupying the position of honor.

THE TEA-TABLE

Perhaps more important than the tea itself, is the appearance of the tea-table. The well-equipped table is adorned with fine china and gleaming silver, and there are always a few flowers to add to the beauty of the setting. Ferns may be used instead of flowers, but there must be no elaborate ribbons or decorations such as appear on the dinner-table.

As a matter of fact, the tea-table should always present an appearance of unpremeditated simplicity. It must never seem as though it had been especially prepared and planned for the occasion. Candles, dimmed with pale shades, may be on the table when the day is gloomy and dark. In winter, for instance, when the days are shorter, softly-glowing candles aid considerably in the cheerfulness of the afternoon tea. Tea napkins are used instead of those of regular dinner size.

A pretty manner of serving sandwiches or cakes is to have them in silver-rimmed wicker baskets which can be passed easily from one guest to another. If the tea is informal, wicker chairs and tables may also be used. This

TEAS AND OTHER ENTERTAINMENTS 61

is especially pleasing and appropriate when the tea is served on the porch or in the garden.

DRESS AT TEA TIME

Tea time is always the fashionable time of the day and there is sufficient variety in appropriate materials and style for a woman to find a gown that is more than ordinarily individual and becoming. For an informal tea the hostess may wear a clinging gown of silk but she should not dress very sumptuously for her guests will come simply attired and it is hardly hospitable to be a great deal more elaborately dressed than they. Afternoon frocks of silk, velvet, cloth, etc., or of summer materials are suitable for the guest. When the weather demands it she wears an attractive wrap.

In selecting dresses for teas, and, indeed for all occasions, it is well to remember that the more ornamentation there is the less elegance there will be. The materials should be rich but not showy—the best-dressed person is the one who calls least attention to his or her clothes.

One may wear jewels but not heavy necklaces or glittering brooches or other flashing stones. If the affair is a formal one the hair may be as elaborately marcelled as for the evening. In this case the gown should be a rich creation of the kind suitable only for such events.

If the tea is given for a *débutante* it may be a very festive occasion and *décolleté* gowns may be worn. Dark colors are rarely worn and the *débutante* herself should be a fairy dream in a lovely creation of silk, georgette, *crêpe-de-chine*, or something else equally girlish and appropriate.

Elderly women wear black lace or satin though certain

BOOK OF ETIQUETTE

shades of brown and blue and nearly all shades of gray are irreproachably good taste if—and this "if" is an important one—they are becoming.

THE GARDEN PARTY

Charming indeed is the simple entertainment of the garden party. It is an undebatable fact that informal entertainments are always more enjoyable than those that are strictly formal, and the easy harmony of the garden party is certainly informal to an acceptable degree.

Someone once said of the lawn fête (which is merely another name for a garden party) that "a green lawn, a few trees, a fine day and something to eat" constitute a perfect garden party. To this we add, that the guests must be carefully selected and the grounds must be attractive.

The garden party must be held in the open air; refreshments are served outside and the guests remain outside until they are ready to depart. At Newport, where garden parties are quite the vogue, the invitations are sent weeks in advance, and, if the weather is bad, the party is held indoors. But ordinarily it must be held entirely on the grounds. A large porch is a great advantage, for if there is a sudden downpour of rain, the guests may repair to its shelter.

There are many opportunities for the hostess to show consideration and hospitality at the garden party. Easy chairs arranged in groups or couples under spreading trees always make for comfort. Some hostesses have a tent provided on the lawn for the purpose of serving the refreshments—a custom which earns the approbation of

TEAS AND OTHER ENTERTAINMENTS 63

fastidious guests who search the food for imaginary specks of dust when it is served in the open.

RECEIVING THE GUESTS

Invitations to garden parties may be sent ten days to two weeks in advance, and a prompt reply of acceptance or regret is expected. The hostess receives on the lawn—never in the house. The guests, however, drive up to the door of the house, are directed upstairs to deposit their wraps (if they wish they may keep them with them), and then are shown to the part of the grounds where the hostess is receiving. A servant should be in attendance to see that each guest is properly directed, unless the grounds where the hostess is receiving are visible from the house.

After being greeted by the hostess, guests may wander about the grounds, stopping to chat with different groups, and seeking the refreshment table when they are weary. The hostess must be sure that her lawns are faultlessly mowed, and that the tennis courts are in order. Lawn-tennis has had a large share in the making of the garden party's popularity, and the wise hostess will always be sure that her courts are in readiness for those who enjoy the game.

Cold refreshments are usually served at the garden party. Salads, ham and tongue sandwiches, fruits, jellies, ices, cakes, candies and punch are in order. Particular care must be taken in serving the refreshments to avoid any accidents or mussiness. There is nothing more disturbing to both hostess and guest than to have a glass of punch or a dish of strawberries overturned on

64 BOOK OF ETIQUETTE

a lawn, and pains should be taken to avoid accidents of this kind.

ON THE LAWN

Music is a pleasing feature at the garden party. A pretty custom, now enjoying vogue among the most fashionable, is to have the orchestra hidden by a clump of trees or shrubbery, but near enough to be heard distinctly. In the outdoors music is never too loud to interfere with conversation, and it is always a source of keen enjoyment to the guests. Also, it adds a solemn charm to the natural beauties of the occasion.

In planning a garden party, it is best to hire all the glass, silver and china from the caterer, as there is always considerable breakage no matter how careful the servants may be. If the hostess does use her own china and glassware, she must never use her best unless she is willing to take the risk of having it broken. Undoubtedly, the garden party is troublesome, but it offers possibilities of tremendous enjoyment and amusement, and when properly arranged is always a success.

The correct time for a garden party is between three and six in the afternoon. Sometimes it lasts until seven if the day is long and the guests are congenial. It rarely lasts into the evening, however, unless it is in celebration of some special event. Sometimes evening lawn receptions are held, and they are remarkably pretty. An appropriate time to hold an evening garden party is in celebration of a summer wedding anniversary. The grounds are brilliantly lighted with many-hued Japanese lanterns or tiny colored electric lights twining in and out among the trees. Benches and chairs are set in groups or pairs

TEAS AND OTHER ENTERTAINMENTS 65

underneath the trees. Music is usually on the porch instead of on the grounds. The house is open, and the younger guests may dance if they wish. Supper is served either outdoors or indoors as convenient. Altogether the garden party, whether held in the afternoon or evening, is a picturesque, charming and delightful affair and deserves the wide popularity it is enjoying both in America and England.

DRESS FOR GARDEN PARTIES AND LAWN FESTIVALS

Summer frocks, in their airy flimsiness and gay colors are ideally fitted for the colorful background of a garden or lawn party. And the lady's escort, in his white trousers and dark sack coat adds still further a note of festivity.

For the garden party, the woman wears her prettiest light-colored frock and flower-trimmed hat. Gay parasols may be carried if they match, or harmonize with, the rest of the costume. Light shoes are more attractive than dark ones with light frocks.

A garden party might be compared with a drama, the costumes of the guests deciding whether or not it would be termed pure romance or light comedy. Here, amidst summer flowers, woman's natural beauty is heightened, and the wrong color schemes in dress, the wrong costumes for the setting, jar as badly as a streak of black paint across the hazy canvas of a landscape painting by an impressionist.

WOMAN'S GARDEN COSTUME

Organdie seems to be the material best suited for the garden-party frock. For the younger person there could

66 BOOK OF ETIQUETTE

be no prettier frock for garden or lawn party, or indeed for any outdoor afternoon occasion.

For the older woman, a dress of dotted Swiss, pierette crêpe, or French lawn is becoming. The color should be light and attractive, but the style may be as simple as one pleases. Lilac is a pretty color for the older woman, and sunset yellow is becoming both to age and youth alike, when it is appropriately combined with some more somber shade.

There are several color combinations that are very beautiful in lawn and garden settings. We will mention them here, as they might be valuable in selecting frocks for such occasions as mentioned. Violet and orange, both pale and not vivid, offer a delicate harmony of color that is nothing short of exquisite. Old rose and Nile green are equally effective. Orchid, for the person whose complexion can bear it, may be combined with such vivid colors as red, green and blue, presenting a contrast so strong and clear and beautiful that it reminds one of a glorious sunset. Black satin, for the elderly person, is quite festive enough for the garden party when it is combined with a pretty shade of henna or old blue or some other bit of color.

Styles may be simple, but colors must always be gay and rich as the colors from Nature's own palette. And the hat that is broad-brimmed and massed with bright flowers, is a fitting complement for such a costume.

THE MAN AT THE GARDEN PARTY

Of course the decorative art of dress has for a long time been entrusted wholly into the hands of woman, but man may be just as attractive on festive occasions, if he

TEAS AND OTHER ENTERTAINMENTS 67

follows the rules of correct dress. For him there is less color to be considered, but just as much effect.

The younger man is well-dressed for the garden party when he wears a suit of white flannel or serge with colored or white linen, a bright tie, straw or panama hat, and oxfords of white or black, or a combination of white and black. Loose jackets of black and white striped flannel may also be worn with white duck trousers, if one is young. Then there are the attractive light suits of gray twillett that are so effective when worn with a white waistcoat and bright tie.

For the older man, a jacket of black and white homespun is extremely appropriate. It is smart when worn with a waistcoat of white flannel, white shirt and collar and gayly figured tie of silk foulard. Trousers of white flannel would complete this excellent costume for the elderly man, and with a panama hat that boasts a black band, and black-and-white oxfords he is ready for the most exclusive garden or lawn party.

HOUSE PARTIES

No one should attempt a house party whose home is not comfortably large enough and who is not able to provide every convenience for the guests. One need not necessarily be a millionaire to hold a successful house party, but it is certainly necessary to have a spacious home and sufficient means to make things pleasant for the guests every minute of the time that they are in the house.

While the success of a house party rests directly on the host and hostess, it also depends largely upon the guests themselves. They are expected to contribute to the entertainment. They may be good conversationalists, or witty humorists, or clever in arranging surprises.

BOOK OF ETIQUETTE

A man or woman who is jolly, eager to please is always invited to house parties and welcomed by both hostess and guests with equal pleasure and cordiality.

SENDING THE INVITATION

The invitations to house parties are important. While it is complimentary for a guest to be invited to "spend a few days with me next week" he or she will undoubtedly be ill at east during the visit and fearful of encroaching upon the hospitality of the hostess. It is always more considerate and better form to state the definite duration of the visit, for instance, mentioning that a train leaves the guest's town at eleven-thirty on a certain day, and that another train leaves *for* that same guest's town, at a certain hour on the day he is to leave. This gives the guest clearly, and without discourtesy, the precise time he is expected to remain at the home of the hostess, and he may remain the full time without any vague premonitions of undesired presence. If the hostess did not state the time of arrival and departure the guest should in her acceptance give suggestive dates leaving them subject to change at the discretion of the hostess. Any other plan is embarrassing to both hostess and guest since neither can make plans for the future until she finds out what the other intends to do.

The usual duration of house party visits are three days —often they last for a week end—although some continue a week or even longer. The lady of the house usually writes a note in the name of her husband and herself both, inviting Mr. and Mrs. Blank to her house for three days or three months as she (the hostess) pleases. A clear explanation as to how to reach the house is given,

TEAS AND OTHER ENTERTAINMENTS 69

and also the necessary information regarding trains and schedules.

These invitations must be answered promptly and if for any reason the invited one cannot attend, the reason should be given. If there is any doubt as to how to get to the house of the hostess; questions may be asked in the answer to the invitation, and the hostess must answer them at once.

WHEN THE GUESTS ARRIVE

If the hostess cannot be present to receive her guests, the duty devolves upon the daughter of the house or an intimate friend. As soon as a guest arrives he is shown to his room for after the long railroad trip one is usually dusty, tired and not in the mood for conversation or pleasantries. A bath, a nap, and a cup of coffee or tea, or, if the weather is warm, an iced drink are most welcome.

The taxi fare from the station may be paid by either hostess or guest. The former may consider that the other is her guest from the moment she arrives and the latter may include this item in her traveling expenses. Generally speaking, the hostess bears all of the expenses of the guest while she is in her home but special services such as laundry work, pressing, etc., may be paid for by the guest herself.

It is bad form to invite numerous friends and then to crowd them two in a room to make a place for all. Of course a mother and daughter may be asked to share the same room if individual beds are provided; but two women, meeting at the house party for the first time, cannot be expected graciously to accept and enjoy sharing the same bed and room together.

BOOK OF ETIQUETTE

The furnishing of the guest chamber may be modest, but it must always be neat and comfortable. To make the visit a pleasant one, the room that the guest will occupy during his stay must be one that invites memory—one that by its very cheerfulness and comfort remains fondly in one's memory. The personal tastes of the guests themselves should be ascertained in assigning rooms to them; some may like a sunny room, others may not be able to endure it; and the considerate hostess will so arrange that each one of her guests is pleased.

There are numerous little services that the hostess must make sure are provided for her visiting guests. Scissors, thread and needles should be in one of the dressing-table drawers; stationery, pens, ink, and a calendar should be in the writing-desk. Books, chosen especially for the occupant, should be scattered about. The thoughtful hostess will make a round of the rooms before the arrival of the guests and make sure that every detail is attended to. Fresh flowers should be placed in the vases.

It is the duty of the guest to see that her room is kept in order. If there is no maid she should attend to it herself and in any case she should keep her own things in place and watch carefully to see that the room is at all times exquisitely neat.

ENTERTAINING AT THE HOUSE PARTY

At eight o'clock, or a little later if it is more convenient, all the guests meet in evening dress at dinner. It is then that the necessary introductions are made and the guest of honor, if there is one, is presented. Plans may be made for the next day or two, the hostess offering suggestions and deferring to the wishes of her guests when they have

TEAS AND OTHER ENTERTAINMENTS 71

attractive plans to submit. The hostess also informs the guests at what time breakfast and luncheon is served. It is not obligatory for every guest to be present at luncheon, but it is strictly so at dinner.

The considerate hostess, while endeavoring to fill every moment of her guests' stay with her, with pleasure and happiness, does not overdo it to the extent that they will have no time for writing their correspondence, reading a bit, or taking their customary nap. Unfortunately many of our hostesses who entertain lavishly at house parties and spare no expense or effort in making the party a brilliant success, spoil it all by trying to crowd too much entertainment into the day, forgetting that their guests need a little time to themselves.

In planning entertainments for the morning, the hostess must remember that breakfast will be preferred late, and that the women guests, especially, may prefer to forego breakfast entirely and keep to their rooms until just before luncheon. Thus it is always best to start any entertainment in the afternoon. Long drives through the country, tennis, hockey, golf, card parties—all these are appropriate for the afternoon.

The evening is usually devoted to some special entertainment prepared sufficiently in advance to render it an important occurrence. A dance after dinner, a fancy dress ball, or private theatricals are suitable; and often long moonlight drives, ending with a jolly little picnic, are planned with great success.

HOSTESS AND GUESTS AT THE HOUSE PARTY

The first duty of the hostess is personally to meet or have her husband meet the guests as they arrive at the

BOOK OF ETIQUETTE

railroad station. It is better form to have him meet them while she remains at home to receive them.

There are several important rules that the guest must observe. In the first place, he must not fail to arrive and depart at the exact time signified in the invitation. If a train is missed, the correct thing to do is wire immediately so that the host and hostess will not be awaiting the arrival in vain. Another important rule for the guest is rigidly to follow and adhere to the laws and the customs of the house: thus if smoking is not allowed in the bedrooms, the gentlemen must be sure to refrain from so doing and each guest should adapt his hours to those of the host and hostess.

One of the most difficult of guests to entertain is one who is peculiar about his eating. It is an awkward situation and the guest if he can should eat what is set before him. If this is impossible he may speak quietly with his hostess, explain the situation and make special arrangements for food that he can eat. This is excusable if he is on a diet prescribed by a physician but not if he is simply expressing a fastidious preference. So many people are vegetarians nowadays that the hostess will make provision for them and she should in planning her menus consult the individual tastes of the guests who are under her roof.

Perhaps a guest is unwisely invited to a house-party where someone he or she particularly dislikes is also a guest. In this case it is a mark of extreme discourtesy to complain to the host or hostess, or in any way to show disrespect or dislike towards the other guest. To purposely ignore him or her, obviously to show one's prejudice, is very rude. It is most disconcerting to the host for either of them to show discontent or to leave the house

TEAS AND OTHER ENTERTAINMENTS 73

party because of the unwelcome presence of the other. It is best for them to be formally courteous to each other and not in any way to interfere with the enjoyment of the other members of the house party or of the host and hostess who are responsible for it.

To return to the hostess, she has two very important duties—not to neglect her guests, but to provide them with ample amusement and entertainment, and again, not to weary them by too much attention. She may go out during the day if she pleases, either to visit friends or to do shopping, but she must always be at home for dinner. And she must not go out so often that the guests will begin to feel slighted.

The good-natured and hospitable host and hostess will put at the disposal of their guests their entire house and grounds, including their books, horses, cars, tennis courts and golf links. The duty of the guest is to avail himself of these privileges with delicacy, neither abusing them nor hesitating to use them at all. There are some guests who have a tact of perception, an ease and poise of manner, a *savoir faire* and calm, kind disposition that makes them welcome everywhere. They are never petty, never disagreeable, never quarrelsome, never grouchy. It is a pleasure to include them in the house party—and they *are* invariably included.

"TIPPING" THE SERVANTS

The question of feeing or "tipping" the servants has always been a puzzling one. It may be of advantage here to give an approximate idea of what the fees should be and to whom they should be given. Attending circumstances, of course, always govern the exact conditions.

BOOK OF ETIQUETTE

Very often guests, both men and women, unable to estimate correctly what amount is befitting the servants' services, tip lavishly and without any regard for services. This borders on the ostentatious, and hence, may be considered vulgar.

Here are the recognized tips expected of a single woman: for the maid who keeps her room in order, one dollar or a dollar and a half. (These figures are based on a period of a week's stay). If this maid has also helped the guest in her dressing, and preparing the bath for her, two or two and a half dollars are the customary fee. A tip of from one to two dollars must be given to the maid who waits on the guest at the table, and if a chauffeur takes her from and to the station, a dollar is his usual fee.

A bachelor is expected to be somewhat more generous with his tips. The boy who cleans and polishes his boots and shoes receives a fee of fifty or seventy-five cents.

When a married couple is visiting, they usually divide the tips between them. The wife gives the maid a dollar or a dollar and a half, and the husband tips the men servants. The butler should receive two dollars at least, and if he has rendered many special services both to the man and his wife, he should undoubtedly receive two or three dollars more. On some occasions the cook is remembered, and the gentleman sends her a dollar or two in recognition of her culinary art. It must be remembered, however, that there are no established rules of tipping, and no precedent to go by. One must be guided by the extent of his income and by the services rendered.

One more word in closing this chapter. Not everyone can afford to give elaborate house parties. But this need not interfere with one's hospitality. The host or hostess who is discouraged from offering friends simple entertain-

TEAS AND OTHER ENTERTAINMENTS   75

ment because of someone's else magnificent parties, should cease being discouraged and take pride and pleasure in the knowledge that they are entertaining their friends as hospitably as they can. To do a thing simply and sincerely is infinitely finer than to do a thing extravagantly merely for the sake of ostentation and display.

In homes where there are no servants the guests should take part in the work around the house unless the hostess shows distinctly that she prefers for them not to do it. After the visit the guest may send some little gift in appreciation of the hospitality enjoyed. A bit of household linen, a book, flowers, or candy are most appropriate. This is one case where an unsuitable gift is inexcusable for ample opportunity has been given the donor to study the needs and desires of the hostess.

Within ten days after her departure the guest should write a bread-and-butter letter to her hostess. This is simply a grateful expression of appreciation for the hospitality which she enjoyed during her visit. Great care should be taken to avoid stilted forms.

CHAPTER V

WHEN THE BACHELOR ENTERTAINS

WHEN THE BACHELOR IS HOST

Until very recently, the bachelor was rarely a host, was rarely expected to entertain. In fact, some people considered it unconventional to attend a bachelor entertainment. But with the tremendous increase of bachelor apartments and bachelor hotels and even bachelor clubs, it is now quite the usual custom for him to entertain friends at dinner parties, theater parties, teas and in almost any other way which strikes his fancy.

However, no bachelor should invite guests to his home unless he has a full retinue of servants to care for their wants. There should be no confusion, no awkwardness. If he is a professional man—an artist, author or musician—he may entertain guests at his studio without servants, except perhaps one to attend to the buffet supper which is most usual at such functions. But that is the only exception; a large entertainment in a bachelor's establishment requires as careful preparation as a fashionable social function in a well-regulated household.

When an unmarried man gives house parties, dinners or entertainments of any kind whatever, he always asks a

WHEN THE BACHELOR ENTERTAINS 77

married woman of his acquaintance to act as chaperon. She should be the first person invited, and the usual method of invitation is a personal call at her home.

WELCOMING THE GUESTS

The host receives his guests at the door, welcoming each one with outstretched hand, and introducing immediately to the chaperon or chaperons those guests whom they do not already know. When the reception is a particularly large one, a man servant usually awaits the guests at the door and the host receives in the drawing-room.

The question has arisen on various occasions, whether or not the bachelor is expected to provide dressing-rooms for his guests. If as many as thirty or forty are expected the bed-rooms may be made to serve the purpose of dressing-rooms for the evening. The matter is one entirely dependent upon circumstances and convenience when the entertainment is held in the home of the bachelor himself; but when a large entertainment is given in a hall, dressing-rooms are of course essential.

Very often, when the reception is held in the bachelor's own apartments, where there is only one servant, the chaperon is asked to pour the tea while the host himself serves it. This is a very pretty custom; it certainly lends dignity and impressiveness to the bachelor entertainment to see a charming, matron at the head of the table. And by having the bachelor himself serve the refreshments, a certain companionship and friendliness is created among the guests.

BOOK OF ETIQUETTE

THE BACHELOR'S DINNER

Although he is not expected to retaliate in the matter of invitations to dinners and luncheons, the bachelor often gives dinner parties. For the host is no less eager to entertain than the hostess, and many unmarried men find keen pleasure in gathering their friends about them for a pleasant evening.

In detail, the bachelor's dinner, formal or informal, is very much like the ordinary dinner. The same holds true of the luncheon or supper party. The menu may be identical, if he pleases; but often an elaborate Chinese, French or Italian menu is decided upon as a novelty.

If the guests are all gentlemen, one butler may attend to all their wants, including the serving of the courses. But if there are ladies in the party, the chaperon must be present, and perhaps one or two white-capped maids to serve the dinner.

If the dinner is given in honor of a lady, her seat is always at the right of the host at the table. If there is no guest of honor, this place is filled by the matron who is serving as chaperon.

It is she who makes the first move to leave the dining-room.

The host must extend cordial thanks to the chaperon when she is ready to depart. It is usually upon her good judgment and influence that the success of the dinner depends, and surely the host owes her a debt of gratitude if everything has run smoothly and pleasantly. He also bids his guests a cordial adieu and graciously accepts their thanks for a pleasant evening.

Music is often provided for the entertainment of the

WHEN THE BACHELOR ENTERTAINS 79

guests after a dinner-party. It is not unusual for the host to obtain the services of well-known professional singers and players for the evening.

TEA AT A BACHELOR APARTMENT

The bachelor who feels that he must be hospitable to his friends and entertain them at his home, may safely choose the afternoon tea without apprehension as it is the simplest of entertainments. Of course a chaperon is necessary, as she is at all his entertainments; but there is less restraint and less formality at a tea than at almost any other social function.

Invitations should be issued a week or ten days before the day set for the tea. Guests may include both sexes; but if there are only gentlemen, they may be invited verbally. The tea is served in the dining-room, or if he wishes, the host may have small tea tables laid out in the drawing-room. A silver tea service is always attractive and pleasing, and the host may pour the beverage if the guests are all gentlemen. If ladies are present, either the chaperon may pour, or a servant. Refreshments should consist of delicate sandwiches, assorted cakes and wafers, salted almonds, confections and tea. If there are some among the guests who do not drink tea, chocolate may be served.

As they depart the bachelor host accompanies each one of his guests to the door bidding him or her a cordial good-by. The chaperon must be especially thanked for her service and shown particular deference. Indeed, her host should accompany her after the reception, to her own door if she is without car or escort.

BOOK OF ETIQUETTE

THE BACHELOR DANCE

Wealthy bachelors find pleasure and diversion in giving huge balls and dances. Dinner or a midnight supper may be a delightful adjunct to the dance. A fashionable ball of this kind is sometimes given for the important purpose of introducing a young sister or another relative to society.

The ball is rarely, if ever, held in the bachelor's own apartments. He hires a hall for the occasion, and arranges with several of his married friends to act as chaperons. They also receive with him and help him introduce the guests. As these arrive, they divest themselves of their wraps, in the dressing-rooms provided for the purpose, and then are received in the ballroom by the host and the chaperons. Introductions are made, and the music and dancing begins.

There are not very many bachelors who can entertain in this lavish fashion; but the simpler entertainments, if they have the correct spirit of cordial hospitality, go a long way in establishing the desired relationship between the host and his friends. After all, it is the little things that count; and little courtesies may fittingly repay elaborate ceremonials and fashionable functions, if they are offered in sincere friendliness and warmth.

THEATER PARTIES

Always a favorite with the bachelor, the theater party has recently become his main forte. First in importance, of course, is the selection of a play, a matter which is largely determined by the kinds of visitors the host intends

WHEN THE BACHELOR ENTERTAINS 81

to invite. There is nothing more disturbing than to invite one's friends to a play, and then to feel that they have not enjoyed it. In selecting something light and amusing, or else the performance of some celebrated star, the host is comparatively sure of pleasing most of his guests.

Another important point is to bring together only congenial people for the theater party. One person out of harmony with the rest will spoil the whole evening as certainly as a sudden summer shower spoils the most elaborately planned garden party. It is important to select only those people whose tastes and temperaments blend.

Invitations are informal. A brief, cordial note handwritten on personal stationery is preferred, although some men like to use their club stationery. The name of the play may be mentioned in the invitation. An immediate response is expected, as the host must be given sufficient time to choose another guest, if for some reason, the one invited cannot attend. Men and women may be invited to the theater party, and if there are married couples in the party, a chaperon is not particularly necessary.

YACHTING PARTIES

When a bachelor invites several men and women friends to dine on his yacht, or to take a short cruise, it is absolutely bad form to omit the chaperon. She must be a married woman, and she may join the party with or without her husband. Another important point regarding yachting parties; the host must supply a gig or rowboat to carry his guests to and from the shore, and he must stand on the gangway to greet each one as he arrives, and assist him to the deck of the yacht.

BOOK OF ETIQUETTE

In giving entertainments, the bachelor must remember that no special social obligations are expected of him. He need not be lavish in his dinners and parties, unless he wishes to and can afford it. Simple entertainments, given in the spirit of good fellowship and hospitality, are always appreciated and tend to substantially strengthen friendships.

CHAPTER VI

MUSICALES AND PRIVATE THEATRICALS

PREPARATIONS FOR THE MUSICALE

The only time that music is not subordinated to other purposes of the evening's gathering, is at the musicale. Here it is the sole entertainment of the evening, and it reigns supreme.

In preparing for a musicale, invitations should be engraved and issued at least ten days in advance of the time chosen for the occasion. In inviting her guests, the hostess must be sure that she includes only those among her friends and acquaintances who understand and appreciate good music, and who enjoy it for itself alone. It is not wise to include people who are not fond of music (if there really are any such people!) for they are likely to be bored, and instead of listening quietly to the selections, talk and fidget and so disturb the other guests who are anxious to give their undivided attention to the musicians.

The invitations to a musicale require prompt answers. The third person should be used in both invitations and answers, as the occasion is strictly a formal one.

The drawing-room, in which the musicale is ordinarily held, should be bare of all unnecessary furniture save the piano, chairs for the performers, and seats for the guests. Programs may be printed sufficiently in advance to distribute at the musicale; they always serve as appropriate mementos.

BOOK OF ETIQUETTE

THE AFTERNOON MUSICALE

The usual time for the afternoon musicale is from four to six. It is considerably less formal than a similar affair in the evening, although still requiring strictly formal third-person etiquette in invitations and replies.

It is usual, in issuing invitations for musicales, whether held in afternoon or evening, to have the word "Music" engraved in the lower left-hand corner. If a famous musician is to play his name may appear on the invitation.

The musical selections include various numbers to suit the tastes of the hostess, and those of her guests if she happens to know what they are. Sometimes there are vocal selections in addition to the instrumental selections. All professional singers and players are paid for their services, unless they themselves offer them free. It is very bad form indeed, to invite a singer or player as a guest, and then expect him to give his services. And yet it is done so often, by hostesses who think that they are following the dictates of etiquette to the highest letter of its law! If the performers are friends of the hostess she should present each one with a gift of some sort as an expression of her gratitude for their services.

The lighter music should always be played first, retaining the important numbers for the end. Many hostesses, when they have a famous professional for the afternoon's entertainment, start the musicale with singing or playing by unimportant persons, and end it with the performance of the celebrated professional. It is always pleasing to the guests—and also the professional himself.

The hostess, in receiving her guests, stands in the drawing-room and greets each one as he or she arrives.

MUSICALES AND PRIVATE THEATRICALS 85

When the music begins, she seats herself near the door, and whenever a tardy guest arrives, sees that he is comfortably seated. Incidentally, it is bad form to come late to a musicale; it is disturbing to the performers and guests alike.

Guests do not remain long after the afternoon musicale. The chairs are removed from the drawing-room and ices, punch, little cakes and bonbons are served. As the guests leave, it is customary for them to thank the hostess for her entertainment.

THE EVENING MUSICALE

Similar in general aspect is the evening musicale and yet there are several details that are strikingly different.

It may be held any time in the evening. Again the hostess receives in the drawing-room, and again the selections may be either vocal or instrumental. But the general appearance of the entire affair is more ceremonious, more formal. And after the musicale, instead of simple refreshments, an elaborate supper is usually given.

This supper may consist of jellied bouillon, roast meats, salads, ices, confections, punches and coffee. If an important singer or player contributes to the share of the evening's entertainment he is invited to join the guests. After supper the guests converse for a half hour or so, and depart.

CARD PARTIES AT THE MUSICALE

Very often, instead of giving a dinner, a hostess will arrange several small tables at which four guests can be comfortably seated. She will serve light refreshments,

BOOK OF ETIQUETTE

such as dainty sandwiches, salads, muffins, bouillon and perhaps ices or coffee. After the light repast, the tables will be cleared and cards brought out.

If the hostess decides to have cards, after the musicale, she must mention it in the invitation. The guests may attend only the musicale, if they wish, and leave when the other guests begin the card game. But if the musicale is held in the evening, and supper is served, the guest who remains must also remain for the card games as a matter of courtesy and politeness. If he does not wish to play he may watch the others and join in the conversation during the intervals between games.

DUTIES OF GUESTS AT MUSICALES

The one important rule of conduct at the musicale is to maintain absolute silence during the selections. It is an unforgivable breach of etiquette to speak, fidget or otherwise disturb the guests while the numbers are being performed. Encores are permissible, but loud applause is undeniably vulgar. Silence, interest and attention characterize the ideal guest at the private concert.

Another duty of the guest is to be prompt. It is very disagreeable to the performers, and to the hostess, to have guests arrive late and disturb everyone. However, if one is unavoidably late, to offer profuse apologies, while the musicians are performing, is to make matters worse by prolonging the disturbance. Instead the guest should nod, take his or her seat, and after the musicale, seek out the hostess and offer apologies for not having been on time.

In taking leave of the hostess, cordial thanks for her entertainment are in order. Remarks about the playing of the guests are not very good form, especially if they

MUSICALES AND PRIVATE THEATRICALS 87

are in adverse criticism. A word of sincere praise, however, is never amiss.

DRESS AT THE MUSICALE

Dress at the musicale is essentially what it would be if the occasion were an elaborate reception, and if it is given in the evening formal evening dress is worn. In the summer this convention may be set aside in favor of comfort.

ARRANGING PRIVATE THEATRICALS

Everyone enjoys private theatricals, amateur and otherwise—the hostess, the guests, and the actors and actresses themselves. It is an ideal means of entertainment.

In arranging a private theatrical, which is almost invariably an amateur venture, the first important thing to do is to find a play which is adapted to that talent which is available. It is wise to appoint a committee to read numerous plays and select for final consideration those that seem best fitted to the type of actors and actresses available. If one of the young men is naturally witty and bubbling over with hilarity and good fun, he must not be given a part that necessitates grave and solemn behavior. If he, and the other actors, are given parts not suited to them, the play is doomed to failure before it is even staged.

Unless the performers have had some experience in theatricals it is best to choose a comedy—for even a Greek tragedy in all its poignant simplicity may become a farce in the hands of unskilful actors.

Rehearsals are of vital importance. The members of the cast must rehearse and rehearse and rehearse again

BOOK OF ETIQUETTE

until they know their parts perfectly. They must be punctual and regular in their attendance of the rehearsals; continually to miss them is to spoil the play and a lack of preparation on the part of one actor is unfair to the others, for ultimate success depends on each one of the players.

The performance is usually given in the drawing-room of the host who issues the invitations, which, by the way, must be sent out two or three weeks in advance. The host must arrange for stage, lighting effects, seating facilities and all the other incidental details.

THE PLAYERS

In assigning parts care must be taken, as was pointed out above, in selecting that character which is most in accord with the player's own character. This is so important that it cannot be overemphasized. And when finally the correct part is chosen for him, he must learn his lines so thoroughly that he will be able, figuratively, to "say them in his sleep."

Costumes for the play may be obtained from any theatrical supply house. They must be of the style prevalent at the date of the play; Colonial clothes in a Mid-Victorian setting foredoom the play to failure. A curtain may also be hired from a theatrical supply house, but it is very simple to adjust one made at home by means of brass rings such as are used in hanging portières. There should be a separation in the center so that the curtain may be drawn back from both sides.

Footlights may consist of a row of small electric lights, or a row of reflector lamps will impart the desired effect to the improvised stage. For wings, large Japanese screens

MUSICALES AND PRIVATE THEATRICALS 89

will do or they, too, may be hired from the people who supply the costumes.

To give the effect of lightning, a magnesia torch is most effective. Thunder is simulated by beating slowly on a bass drum. Hoof beats seem quite real when produced by beating two cocoanut shells on marble.

The danger of stage fright can be lessened and almost obliterated after a sufficient number of rehearsals, and with that poise and self-confidence that comes with true culture, one should be able to stand before the largest audience without embarrassment or nervousness. It is one of the rewards of correct training.

THE GUESTS

As in the musicale, silence is essential. There is nothing more disconcerting to actors than to notice whispering, giggling or lack of interest in the audience. Whether the play is worthy of interest or not, courtesy towards guests and performers demands the appearance of interest.

Guests must answer invitations promptly. In fact, in almost every detail, attending a theatrical given in the home of a friend requires the same etiquette as is observed at a fashionable evening musicale. In departing, the hostess must be cordially thanked for the pleasant evening, and if the actors are friends of the assemblage and join the guests after the play, they, too, must be thanked for their share of the entertainment.

HOST AND HOSTESS

The host and hostess usually receive together at private theatricals. They stand together at the door of the draw-

90 BOOK OF ETIQUETTE

ing-room, welcome each guest and make the necessary introductions. When the curtain is drawn, they take seats near the back and rise to greet any delinquent guest.

After the play a supper may be served. If the actors are friends they join in the supper. But sometimes these private theatricals are not amateurish, but given by professionals, in which case the etiquette is somewhat different, and the performers may or may not be invited, as the hostess chooses.

Engraved cards are issued, and in the lower left-hand corner appears the name of the play and the leading actor (if he happens to be a celebrity). The guests are expected to arrive at a definite hour, and lateness in this case is inexcusable. If the professional players do not offer their services free, they must receive remuneration for them.

CHAPTER VII

DANCING

DANCING AS A HEALTHFUL ART

Dancing is an art. More than that, it is a healthful art. In its graceful movements, cadenced rhythms, and expressive charms are evident the same beautiful emotions that are so eloquently expressed in music, sculpture, painting. And it is through these expressions of emotion, through this silent poetry of the body that dancing becomes a healthful art, for it imparts to the body—and mind—a poise and strength without which no one can be quite happy.

It is because the vital importance of dancing on the mind and body has been universally recognized, that it has been added to the curriculum of public schools in almost every country. We find the youngsters revelling in folk-dances, and entering dancing games with a spirit that gives vigor to their bodies, balance and grace to their movements.

Consider, for a moment, the irresistible witchery of music, of rhythmic cadences. We hear the martial note of the drum, and unconsciously our feet beat time. We hear the first deep chords of the orchestra, and involuntarily our fingers mark the time of the measure. With the soft, mellow harmony of triplet melodies we are transported to the solemn vastness of a mountain beside a gayly rippling

BOOK OF ETIQUETTE

stream. With the deep, sonorous bursts of triumphant melody, we are transported to the ocean's edge, where the rumbling of the waves holds us in awed ecstasy. Thoughts of sorrow, of gladness, of joy, of hope surge through us and cry for expression. Dancing is nature's way of expressing these emotions.

Then let us dance, for in dancing we find poise and strength and balance. Let us dance for in dancing we find joy, pleasure, hope. It is the language of the feelings, and nature meant it for the expression of those feelings.

It is only when dancing is confined to hot, crowded rooms where the atmosphere is unwholesome, that it loses its healthful influence on mind and body. But where there is plenty of room and fresh air, plenty of good, soul-inspiring music—we say dance, young and old alike, dance for the keen pleasure and joy of the dance itself, and for the health that follows in its wake!

DANCE-GIVING NO LONGER A LUXURY

The day of the strictly formal dance, entailing elaborate suppers, pretentious decorations and large orchestras has passed. In its place is the simple, enjoyable, inexpensive dance which is at once the delight of the guests and the pride of the hostess.

Simplicity is the keynote of the modern ball. A piano and two stringed instruments usually comprise the entire orchestra. The charm of the home is no longer spoiled by overdecoration; a vase or two containing the flowers of the season offer the sole touch of festivity. There are, of course, numerous personal innovations that may be instituted; but as the guests are assembled for dancing, space

DANCING

and a good floor and plenty of fresh air are the primary and paramount requisites.

Light refreshments have taken the place of the large suppers of not so long ago. Hostesses no longer feel overburdened with a sense of obligation. The dance has become simple and inexpensive; and because it is also so thoroughly enjoyable and healthful, it has become a favorite sport, especially during the cooler months.

THE DEBUT DANCE

Perhaps the most important dance of all is that given in honor of the *débutante*. No matter how large or formal a dance may be, it is never called a "ball" in the invitation. The latter is used only in case of a large public dance or function. The usual "at home" form of invitation is used, and in the lower left-hand corner the word *dancing* is printed. The name of the young *débutante* may be included if it is so desired, although it is not essential. But if it is an evening occasion, the name of both host and hostess must appear on the invitation.

Whether the dance is held in her own home or in a hall hired for the occasion, the hostess receives and welcomes each guest. She may be assisted by several of her friends who are well-known in society. Her daughter stands beside her and is introduced to those of her mother's guests whom she has not already met.

The *débutante* has her first partner selected for her by her mother. She may not dance with one man more than once on the occasion of her introduction to society. But she is expected to dance every dance, returning to receive guests during the intervals. Sometimes the young *débu-*

BOOK OF ETIQUETTE

tante has several of her chums receiving with her for the first half hour. She offers her hand to every guest who arrives, and introduces in turn the friends who are assisting her.

The father of the *débutante* may receive with his wife, but his duty is more to see that all the women have partners, and that the chaperons are taken into supper. He also sees that the gentlemen do their duty as dancers instead of remaining in the dressing room to smoke and chat. The hostess does not dance at all, or if she does, it is usually late in the evening. She remains at her post at the door, welcoming guests and seeing that all shy men get partners and all the young girls have a good time. One paramount duty of the hostess is so to arrange her invitations that there will be very many more men than women; this eliminates the chance of there being any unhappy wallflowers. Another consideration is to arrange the chairs in informal little groups instead of close to the walls in a solemn and dreary line.

COSTUME BALLS

The costume ball is conducted very much on the same order as the formal ball. The invitations are issued two or three weeks before the date set for the dance, and as for the *début* dance, the word *ball* does not appear on it. Instead the words "Costumes of the Twelfth Century" or "Shakespearean Costumes" or whatever may be decided upon are printed in the lower left-hand corner of usual "at home" cards.

In selecting a fancy costume, one must be careful to choose only what is *individually* becoming. It must be in

DANCING 95

perfect harmony with one's personality. To assume a character that is in every way opposed to one's own character is unwise and ungratifying. A sedate, quiet young miss should not choose a Folly Costume. Nor should a jolly, vivacious young lady elect to emulate Martha Washington. And furthermore, a character must not be merely dressed—it must be *lived*. The successful costume ball must be realistic.

SUBSCRIPTION DANCES

What is the purpose of the subscription dance? The question is a common one. And the answer is simple.

A subscription dance is given for the same reason that any other dance is given—to be surrounded by one's friends, to enjoy music and dancing, and generally to have a "good time." It is conducted very much on the order of the formal dance, except that it is semi-public and is usually held in a public hall. There is no host or hostess, of course; their place is held by an appointed committee or by the patronesses of the dance. They stand at the door of the ballroom to welcome guests, and they may either offer their hands or bow in greeting. It is the duty of the patronesses to introduce those of the guests who are not already acquainted.

Each subscriber to the dance has the privilege of inviting a certain number of friends to the function. Or, if the membership decide to give several periodic dances, he is entitled to invite a certain number of friends to each one of them. The invitations are issued two weeks ahead and require a prompt acceptance or regrets.

Sometimes elaborate suppers are served at the sub-

96 BOOK OF ETIQUETTE

scription dance, the money for the expenses having been appropriated from the subscription fees for the entertainment. Or simple refreshments, such as dainty sandwiches, salads, ices, cakes and punch, may be served at small, round tables.

In departing, it is not considered necessary to take leave of the patronesses. However, if they are on duty at the door, a cordial word or two of consideration for their efforts may be extended.

THE BALLROOM

Everything in the ballroom should suggest gayety, light and beauty. The floor, of course, is the most important detail. A polished hardwood floor offers the most pleasing surface for dancing. If the wood seems sticky, paraffine wax adds a smoothness that actually tempts one to dance.

Flowers are always pleasing. Huge ferns may grace unexpected corners and greens may add a festive note, if the hostess so desires. But there must not be an obvious attempt at decoration. Rather nothing at all, than so very much that it borders on the ostentatious.

In fact, the dance is tending more and more to become a simple and unpretentious function. The elaborate decorations and fashionable conventions that attended the minuet and quadrille of several decades ago have given way to a jolly informality which makes the dance so delightful and popular a way of entertaining.

MUSIC AT THE DANCE

The music, of course, is important. A piano and one or two stringed instruments are sufficient. The musicians

DANCING 97

should be hidden behind a cluster of palms, or placed in a balcony.

Ordinarily the selections are arranged previously by the hostess. She must also arrange for encores, and should make provision for special selections which the guests may desire.

DANCE PROGRAMS

The dance program is rarely used now except at college dances, or army and navy dances. It has lost prestige with the passing of the old-fashioned ball. But sometimes there are special occasions when the hostess wishes to have programs, in which case they serve not only as pretty and convenient adjuncts to the occasion, but as appropriate mementos.

Gilt-edged cards attached with a silk cord and provided with a tiny pencil are pretty when an attractive little sketch or a bit of verse enlivens the front cover. Each dance is entered on the program—and many a delightful memory is kept alive by glancing at these names days after the dance was held. These programs may be filled beforehand or they may be filled at the dance.

DINNER DANCES

At the dinner dance, the hostess issues two sets of invitations, one for those whom she wishes to invite for dinner and dance both, and one for those whom she wishes to invite to the dance only. For the former the ordinary dinner invitation may be issued, with the words "Dancing at Nine" added in the left-hand corner. For the latter,

BOOK OF ETIQUETTE

the ordinary "at home" invitation with the same words "Dancing at Nine" added also in the left-hand corner is correct form.

Often the hostess has a buffet supper instead of a dinner. All the guests partake of this refreshment. On a long table, decorated with flowers, are salads, sandwiches, ices, jellies and fruits which may be partaken of throughout the entire evening. Sometimes hot bouillon is also served, and very often a midnight supper is given at which hot courses are in order.

If a dance is scheduled to be held in the ballroom of a hotel, the guests who are invited to dinner may be served in the dining-room of that hotel. The small tables are usually decorated with lamps and flowers for the occasion, and the dinner may be ordered by the hostess several days in advance.

DRESSING ROOMS

Whether the dance be large or small, dressing rooms, or coat rooms, as they are sometimes called, are essential for the convenience of the guests. There must be one for the gentlemen and one for the ladies, each properly furnished.

It is usual to have a maid servant in attendance in the dressing room set apart for the ladies. She helps them relieve themselves of their wraps when they arrive, and to don them again when they are ready to depart. A dressing-table, completely furnished with hand-mirror, powder, perfume and a small lamp, should be provided. A full-size mirror is always appreciated. Sometimes, when a great number of guests are expected, a checking system is devised to simplify matters and aid the maid in identifying the wraps.

DANCING

The men's dressing room may be provided with a smoking table supplied with all the necessary requisites for smoking, matches, ash-trays, cigar-cutters, etc. Here also a servant is usually on hand to offer the gentleman his service wherever it is needed.

THE DANCE

There is a lesser formality, a greater gayety in the ballroom of to-day. The dance-card and program are no longer enjoying unrivaled vogue as they did when our grandmothers' danced the waltz and cotillon. The pauses between dances are shorter. Something of the old dignity is gone, but in its place is a new romance that is perhaps more gratifying. It is not a romance of the Mid-Victorian period, or a romance that carries with it the breath of mystery. It is a strangely companionable and level-headed romance which pervades the ballroom and makes everyone, young and old, man and woman, want to get out on the floor and dance to the tune of the pretty melodies.

But the ballroom of good society, must retain its dignity even while it indulges in the new "romance of the dance." It must observe certain little rules of good conduct without which it loses all the grace and charm which are the pride and inspiration of the dancing couples. There is, for instance, the etiquette of asking a lady to dance, and accepting the invitation in a manner graciously befitting the well-bred young lady of the twentieth century.

WHEN THE LADY IS ASKED TO DANCE

Before asking anyone else to dance, the gentleman must request the first dance of the lady he escorted to the ball.

100 BOOK OF ETIQUETTE

Then he takes care that she has a partner for each dance, and that she is never left a wallflower while he dances with some other lady.

At the conclusion of the dance, the gentleman thanks the lady for the dance and goes off to find his next partner. The lady does not seek her partner for the next dance, if she has promised it to anyone, but waits until he comes to claim her. A man should never leave a woman standing alone on the floor.

"CUTTING IN"

A modern system of "cutting in" seems to be enjoying a vogue among our young people. While a dance is in progress, a young man may "cut in" and ask the lady to finish the dance with him. If the dance has not been very long in progress, and the young lady wishes to continue it, she may nod and say, "The next time we pass here." The dance continues around the room, and when the couple reach the same place again, the lady leaves her partner and finishes the dance with the young man who has "cut in."

Perhaps this custom of "cutting in" carries with it the merest suggestion of discourtesy, but when we consider the informal gayety of the ballroom, the keen and whole-hearted love of dancing, we can understand why the privilege is extended. Like many another privilege, it becomes distasteful when it is abused.

It is not good form for a couple to dance together so many times as to make themselves conspicuous.

Men should not neglect their duty as dancers because they prefer to smoke or simply to act as spectators.

DANCING 101

DANCING POSITIONS

Dancing has been revolutionized since the day when the German waltz was first introduced to polite society. And it is safe to say that some of our austere granddames would feel righteously indignant if they were suddenly brought back to the ballroom and forced to witness some of the modern dance innovations!

There seems to be an attempt, on the part of the younger generation (although the older generation is not so very far behind!) to achieve absolute freedom of movement, to go through the dance with a certain unrestrained impulsiveness unknown to the minuet or graceful quadrille. These newer dances and dancing interpretations are charming and entertaining; and yet there is the possibility of their becoming vulgar if proper dancing positions are not taken. The position is especially important in the latest dances.

In guiding a lady across the polished floor to the tune of a simple waltz or a gay fox-trot, the gentleman encircles her waist half way with his right arm, laying the palm of his hand lightly just above the waist line. With his left hand, he holds her right at arm's length in the position most comfortable for both of them, taking special care not to hold it in an awkward or ungainly position. His face is always turned slightly to the left, while hers usually faces front or slightly to the right. The girl should place her left arm on her partner's right arm. She must follow him and not try to lead the dance herself.

When the dance requires certain swaying movements, as almost all modern dances do, the lady inclines her body in harmony with that of her partner, and if the proper

BOOK OF ETIQUETTE

care is taken to retain one's poise and dignity, not èven a most exacting chaperon can find fault with the new steps.

WHEN THE GUEST DOES NOT DANCE

Always at a dance, formal or informal, there are guests who do not dance. Usually they are men, for there is rarely a woman who does not know the steps of the latest dances—that is, if she ever does accept invitations at all. But "the guest who does not dance" is one of the unfortunate things the hostess has to put up with at every one of her dances.

And there is rarely ever an excuse for it. Every man who mingles in society at all, who enjoys the company of brilliant women and attractive young ladies, who accepts the invitations of hostesses, is failing in his duty when he offers as an excuse the fact that he doesn't know how to dance—for there are sufficient schools of dancing in every city and town where the latest steps can be learned quickly.

If for any reason, a gentleman does not know how to dance, and does not want to learn, he may make up for it by entertaining the chaperons while their charges are dancing,—conversing with them, walking about with them and escorting them to the refreshment table, and altogether show by his kind attentiveness that he realizes his deficiency and wishes to make up for it. To lounge in the dressing-room, smoking and chatting with other gentlemen is both unfair to the hostess and essentially rude in the matter of ballroom etiquette. The true gentleman would rather decline an invitation than be unfair to his hostess and her guests in this respect.

DANCING 103

PUBLIC DANCES

Very often public dances are given in honor of some special occasion or a celebrated guest. They are very much like private dances, except that a specially appointed committee fulfills the position and duties of the hostess. At most public balls, the committee is composed of men and women who wear badges to indicate their position, and who stand at the door to receive and welcome each guest. These men and women do not dance the first dance, but wait until later in the evening when they are quite sure that all the guests have arrived; and then they are always back at their duty during the intervals between dances.

Guests arriving at a public dance greet the patronesses with a smile of welcome and a word or two, but rarely offer their hands to be shaken unless the ladies serving as patronesses take the initiative. They may stay for one or two dances, or throughout the whole evening, as they prefer; and when departing, it is not necessary to seek out the patronesses and bid them good-by.

Engraved invitations are usually issued three weeks before the date set for the ball. On these cards the names of the patronesses are also engraved. If the entrance to the ball is by purchased ticket, such as is always the case when the ball is given for some charity, the invitations must be preserved and shown at the entrance.

Sometimes a supper is included in the arrangement of the public ball, and in such case a caterer is engaged to attend to all details, including servants. A buffet supper is always the most pleasing and satisfactory as the guests may partake of the foods when they desire and

BOOK OF ETIQUETTE

there is no confusion or interruption to the dance. Hot bouillon, various meats, salads, cakes, ices, fruits and confections are an ideal menu. Coffee or punch is sometimes added.

When a public ball is given in honor of some special person, that person must be met on his arrival and immediately introduced to the women on the reception committee and escorted to the seat reserved for him. He must be attended throughout the evening, introduced to everyone he does not know, and all his wants carefully taken care of. When he departs, he must be escorted to his carriage, and if he is a celebrated personage thanked for his presence—although truly cultured gentlemen prefer not to have this honor paid them.

A public ball is either a tremendous success or a miserable failure. There is no in-between. And the success or failure rests solely on the good judgment and influence of the ladies and gentlemen of the committees, including, of course, those who receive. To mingle freely among the guests, to join in the conversation, to introduce guests to each other and find partners for the "wallflowers"— all these little services tend to arouse a spirit of friendliness and harmony that cannot but result in an evening that will be long remembered in the minds of every guest.

A PLEA FOR DANCING

Lately there has been a great deal of unfavorable criticism directed against the modern dances. There have been newspaper articles condemning the "latest dance fads" as immoral and degrading. There have been speeches and lectures against "shaking and twisting of the body into weird, outlandish contortions." There have

DANCING

been vigorous crusades against dance halls. And all because a few ill-bred, fun-loving, carefree young people wrongly interpreted the new dances in their own way and gave to the steps the vulgar abandon appropriate only to the cheap vaudeville stage or the low dance hall.

Dancing, even the shoulder-shaking, oscillating dancing of to-day, is really not intended to be vulgar or immoral at all, despite the crusades of the anti-immorality dancing committees! What is dancing, after all, if not the expression of one's ideals and emotions? It is only the man or woman with a vulgar mind, with base ideals, who will give a vulgar interpretation to a dance of any kind. But the essentially fine girl, the really well-bred man, the people who, by their poise and dignity have earned for America the envied title of "Republic of the Aristocrats"—they dance these latest creations for the sheer joy of the dance itself, reveling in its newness, enjoying the novelty of its "different" steps, seeing nothing in its slow undulations or brisk little steps, but art—a "jazzy" art, to be sure, but still the beautiful art of dancing.

And so we plead—let the younger generation enjoy its giddy waltzes and brisk-paced fox-trots and fancy new dances just as grandmother, when she was young, was allowed to enjoy the minuet and the slow waltz. They are different, yes, and rather hard to accept after the dignified dances of not so long ago. But they are picturesque, to say the least, and artistic. The gracefully-swaying bodies, keeping step in perfect harmony to the tunes of the newer symphony orchestras, are delightful to watch; and in good society, young men and women can always be trusted to deport themselves with utter grace and poise.

The minuet was decidedly graceful. The old Ger-

106 BOOK OF ETIQUETTE

man waltz with its dreamy, haunting melody was beautiful as it was enjoyable. But they have been relegated into the days of hoop skirts and powdered wigs. To-day the "jazzy" dances are in vogue, and society in its lowest and highest circles is finding intense pleasure in the whirling, swirling dances decreed by fashion as her favorites. Why complain? Perhaps in another year or two, these giddy-paced dances will be "out of style" and in their stead will be solemn, slow dances more graceful and stately than even the minuet of yore.

THE CHARM OF DRESS IN DANCING

Immediately after the Reign of Terror, France was plunged into a reckless round of unrestrained gayety that can come only from love of life and youth and laughter long pent-up. It was as though an avalance of joy had been released; it was in reality the reaction from the terrors and nightmares of those two years of horror. The people were free, free to do as they pleased without the fear of the guillotine ever present; and all France went mad with rejoicing.

It was then that dancing came into its own. Almost overnight huge dance halls sprang up. The homes of wealthy aristocrats who had been sacrificed to the monster guillotine, were converted into places for dancing. Every available inch of space was utilized for the dance. And the more these freed people danced, the more their spirits soared with the joy of life and living, until they found in the dance itself the interpretation of freedom and all that it means.

A biographer who was an eye-witness of this madcap Paris, wrote in detail about the dance and the dress of

DANCING

these people. He told how they dressed in the brightest clothes they could obtain, for maddened with happiness as they were, they instinctively felt that bright clothes would enliven their spirits. And they did!

"The room was a mass of swirling, twirling figures," the biographer writes, "men, women and children in weird, vivid clothes. It seemed natural that they should be dancing so wildly in their wild costumes; in their *sabots* and aprons of two months ago they would not have been able to take one step."

It is, then, the spirit of clothes that imparts to one the spirit of the dance. We have mentioned these facts about the Reign of Terror to show what effect clothes do have on the spirit, and incidentally to show what the ballroom owes to dress. For it is undoubtedly the gayly-colored dance frock of the miss of the twentieth century, and the strikingly immaculate dance suit of her partner that gives to the ballroom to-day much of its splendid brilliance.

AT THE AFTERNOON DANCE

There can be no comparison between the mad dance of freed France and the simple, graceful dance of to-day. Yet we can see the effect of clothes in relation to both.

It is not often that dances are held in the afternoon, but when the occasion does arise, dress is just as gay and colorful as one can wear without being gaudy. The decorous effect of these bright-colored costumes is what brings the "giddy kaleidoscopic whirl of colors and costumes, modes and manners" that the historian speaks of when he mentions the ballroom.

For the afternoon dance, we would suggest that the

BOOK OF ETIQUETTE

very young person choose the fluffiest and most becoming style which fashion permits. Trim it gaily, but above all, make it youthful—for youth and dancing are peculiarly allied.

The older woman will want a gown that is more suited to her years. It may be of taffeta, Canton crêpe or *crêpe-de-chine;* but satin is one of the materials that is preferred for more formal occasions than the afternoon dance. The colors may be somber, to match one's tastes, but the trimming should have a note of gayety.

Décolleté is never worn at the afternoon dance. Short sleeves may be worn if Fashion favors them at the time, and the neck of the gown is also cut on the lines that agree with the prevalent mode. But it is extremely bad taste, even for a very celebrated guest of honor, to attend the afternoon dance in a sleeveless, *décolleté* gown.

A late custom seems to favor the wearing of satin slippers to match the gown. It is not by any means bad taste, but patent leather or kid pumps are preferred for the afternoon, reserving the more elaborate satin pumps for evening wear. Long white silk or kid gloves and a light-colored afternoon wrap complete the correct dress for the afternoon dance. The hat, of course, depends on Fashion's whim at the moment.

GENTLEMEN AT THE DANCE

In summer, the gentleman may wear a complete suit of gray with a white duck waistcoat and light linen to the afternoon dance, completing his costume with black patent leather shoes or oxford ties, light gray gloves, and straw hat with black and white band. But whether it

DANCING

be for summer or winter, the dark suit is always better taste.

It may be of serge, twillet or homespun, preference being given always to the conventional navy blue serge. Double-breasted models are appropriate for the young man; single-breasted for the older. Light linen and bright ties are in full accordance with the gay colors worn by the women at the dance. The coat may be the ordinary unlined, straight hanging overcoat of thin material in a light color, or it may be an attractive full-belted raglan coat of tan or brown fleece. In either case it is worn with the conventional afternoon hat of the season.

DRESS FOR THE BALL

When the dance is held in the evening, it often assumes an air of formality.

It is at the ball that such important events as introducing one's daughter to society or celebrating the graduation of one's son from college, takes place.

Of course, one wears one's most important jewels to the ball, and indulges in a headdress that is a trifle more elaborate than usual. The event is a brilliant one, and if gaudiness and ostentation are conscientiously avoided, one may dress as elaborately as one pleases.

This does not mean, however, that the woman whose purse permits only one evening gown, need feel ill at ease or self-conscious at the ball, for simplicity has a delightful attractiveness all its own, and if the gown is well-made of excellent materials, and in a style and color that is becoming, one will be just as effectively dressed as the much-bejeweled dowager.

BOOK OF ETIQUETTE

DRESS OF THE DÉBUTANTE

A gown is chosen with much premeditated consideration for so momentous an occasion as being ushered into society. The young lady does well to seek the advice of her friends who are already in society, and of her modiste who knows by long experience just what is correct and becoming. But perhaps we can give some advice here that will be helpful.

A delicately tinted gown, in pastel shades, or one that is pure white is preferred for the happy *débutante*. Tulle, chiffon, net and silk georgette are the most popular materials. The style should be youthful and simple, preferably bordering on the bouffant lines rather than on those that are more severely slender. The neck may be cut square, round or heart-shaped, and elbow-length sleeves or full-length lace sleeves are preferred. The sleeveless gown is rarely worn by the young *débutante*.

The *débutante* who wears many jewels displays poor taste. Just a string of softly glowing pearls, or one small diamond brooch, is sufficient. Her hair should be arranged simply in a French coil or youthful coiffure, and should be wholly without ornamentation. Simplicity, in fact, is one of the charms of youth, and the wise young person does not sacrifice it to over-elaboration, even on the day of her *début*.

WRAPS AT THE BALL

The woman wears her most elaborate evening wrap to the ball. Soft materials in light shades are suggested, with trimmings of fur for the winter months. A wrap of

DANCING

old blue or old rose velvet with a collar of white fox is becoming and attractive when it is within one's means. But the simple wrap of cloth, untrimmed, is certainly better taste for the woman whose means are limited. However, discrimination should be shown in the selection of lines and colors. A simple wrap, well-cut, and of fine material in a becoming shade, is as appropriate and effective as a wrap completely of fur. For the woman who must dress economically a dark loose coat of black satin is serviceable for many occasions.

Hats are never worn to the ball. A shawl or scarf of fine lace may be thrown over the hair and shoulders. Or a smaller shawl may be tied merely around the head. Satin pumps are worn, usually with buckle trimmings; and long gloves of white silk or kid, or in a color to match the gown, complete the outfit.

BALL DRESS FOR MEN

Nothing less strictly formal than the complete full dress suit is worn by the gentleman at the evening ball. His costume strikes a somber, yet smart, note.

Whether it be summer or winter, the gentleman wears the black full dress coat, lapels satin-faced if he so desires, and trousers to match. Full rolled waistcoat, small bow-tie and stiff linen are all immaculately white. Patent leather pumps and black silk socks complete the outfit.

In summer, the gentleman wears over his full dress suit a light unlined coat, preferably black in color. If the lapels of the suit are satin-faced, the coat lapels may correspond. White kid gloves are worn, and a conventional silk hat. In winter, the coat may be a heavy, dark-colored raglan, although the Chesterfield overcoat

BOOK OF ETIQUETTE

more suits his dignified dress. With it he wears white kid gloves and a high silk hat or felt Alpine as he prefers.

FOR THE SIMPLE COUNTRY DANCE

There can be nothing more picturesque and delightful than some of the pretty little social dances held in the smaller towns. Sometimes they are held in the afternoon; more often in the evening, but always they are a source of keen enjoyment both to the participants and to those who "look on."

We are going to tell you about a dance held recently in the home of a social leader in a typical small town. Everyone of any consequence whatever attended, and the occasion proved one worthy of remembrance in the social annals of the town. There were perhaps one hundred and fifty women and one hundred men. Three rooms in the hostess' home were thrown open into one huge ballroom. The dancing began at eight o'clock in the evening—rather early for the city, but unusually late for this country town.

To a visitor from so gay a metropolis as New York, the simplicity of the women's dress was a pleasing change. They were in evening dress, yes,—but a strangely more conservative evening dress than that described previously for the formal ball. There were no sleeveless gowns, no elaborate *décolletés*. Taffetas, chiffons and silk brocades were developed simply into gowns of dignified charm. One did not notice individual gowns, for no one woman was dressed more elaborately than another. This is what everyone should strive for—simplicity with charm and a complete absence of all conspicuousness.

Fashion has been condemned. Women have been ridi-

Photo by George H. Davis, Jr.

THE PUNCH TABLE

Courtesy of the *Woman's* Home Companion

DANCING 113

culed for their "extreme tastes." As a matter of fact, civilization owes dress a great debt, and women have an inherent good taste. And both these facts are forcibly proved at the country dance, where simplicity and harmony of color combine to give an effect that is wholly delightful and charming.

The lesson we might take from this is that simplicity in dress has more beauty and effect than elaborate "creations."

CHAPTER VIII

GAMES AND SPORT

WHY THE WORLD PLAYS

All the world loves to play. In childhood, it is the very language of life. In youth, it vies with the sterner business of young manhood or womanhood. When we are older and the days of childhood are but a fading memory, we still have some "hobby" that offers recreation from our business and social duties. It may be golf or tennis or billiards; but it is *play*—and it is a relaxation.

It is a fundamental law of nature that we shall play in proportion to the amount of work we do. The inevitable "tired business man" finds incentive in the thought of a brisk game of golf after closing hours. The busy hostess looks forward to the afternoon that she will be able to devote exclusively to tennis. The man or woman who does not "play" is missing one of the keenest pleasures of life.

But there is an etiquette of sport and games, just as there is an etiquette of the ballroom and dinner table. One must know how to conduct oneself on the golf links and at the chess table, just as one must know how to conduct oneself at dinner or at the opera. And in one's play, one must remember that touching little fable of the frogs who were stoned by boys, in which the poor little creatures cried, "What is play to you is death to us." Be

GAMES AND SPORT 115

kind, unselfish and fair. Do not sacrifice, in the exciting joyousness of the game, the little courtesies of social life. Remember Burns' pretty bit of verse—we cannot resist the temptation of printing it here:

"Pleasures are like poppies spread,
You seize the flower, its bloom is shed;
Or, like the snowfall on the river,
A moment white, then melts forever."

FAIR PLAY

Nothing so quickly betrays a person as unfairness in games. It hardly seems necessary to mention it, to caution anyone against it. Yet so many people are prone to believe that the courtesies we observe in social life, may be entirely forgotten in the world of sport and pleasure—and that with them, we may forget our scruples. "Cheating" is a harsh word and we do not want to use it. But what other word can be used to describe unfairness, to describe selfish discourtesies?

"Fair play is a jewel." This proverb has been handed down to us among other old sayings of the Danish, and Denmark loves its games and sports as few other countries do. It was here that the game of Bridge first had its inception. It was here that the game of "Boston" first won prominence. Many of the games and sports practiced in America to-day had their origin in Denmark. And it was that country that gave to us the golden proverb, "Fair play is a jewel."

We could fill a complete volume on the ethics of sport, but it is not necessary to elaborate on the subject in a book of etiquette. When you are on the tennis courts or at the billiard tables remember only to observe the same

116 BOOK OF ETIQUETTE

good manners and courtesies that characterize your social
life—and you will play fair.

INDOOR GAMES

Bridge and chess have long been the boon of puzzled
hostesses. These indoor games offer a wealth of interest
and enjoyment to visiting guests, and in social circles
they are frequently resorted to, to make an afternoon or
evening pass pleasantly.

Every woman who ever invites people to her home,
should know the etiquette of indoor games. It is also
necessary that she herself know how to play the games,
as it will be expected that she join her guests. At a recent silver wedding the host and hostess evolved the novel
idea of spending the evening playing bridge with the
guests and offering silver prizes to the winners. Everyone enjoyed the evening, and it saved the hostess the
trouble of worrying about providing satisfactory entertainment.

Some women who enjoy indoor games form clubs for
the purpose of devoting one or more afternoons or eve-
nings a week to the favored game. There are numerous
chess and bridge clubs that meet in private homes or in
club-rooms rented for the purpose. The usual method
is to meet at the home of one of the members, rotating
each week so that each member has her turn at being
hostess.

CHESS

There is something romantic, something strangely fan-
ciful in the old game of chess. Its origin is forgotten in
a dim past—a past around which is woven historical tales

GAMES AND SPORT 117

of kings and queens, interesting anecdotes of ancient sports and pleasures. There is perhaps no indoor game as old and as beloved. (See footnote.)*

Chess is also one of the most universal of games. In slightly altered form, it is played in almost every country. Games resembling chess are found even in uncivilized countries. To know the rudiments of the game, is to be able to enter into at least one sport when traveling in other countries.

We trace the origin of chess to the ancient Sanscrit Indians. At that time it was known as "chatauranga." From this word, the word "shatrang" was evolved, developing slowly into our modern word "chess." It was in the sixteenth century that the surface of the chess-board was chequered black and white. Just as the capture of a king by enemies meant the terminating of his rule of the kingdom in those days, the capture of the "king" on the chess-board to-day terminates the game.

It is interesting to note that the different "pieces" used in the game of chess all have their origin in ancient history. The game is one of the most interesting in existence, and the man or woman who does not already know how to play it, should learn how as soon as possible. There are numerous authorities who are only too glad to teach it.

The hostess who plans a chess-party for her guests should arrange a sufficient number of small tables in the drawing- or reception-room. Usually coffee and wafers are served as refreshment in the afternoon; but if the

---

* To inspire interest in certain games, and to give renewed zest to those who have already made one of these games a hobby, it was considered worth-while to give in these chapters the interesting facts regarding the origin of some of our popular modern games. We are indebted to Paul Monckton, whose splendid book, "Pastimes in Times Past" has helped us to make this possible.

118   BOOK OF ETIQUETTE

party is held in the evening, it usually terminates in a cold
midnight supper.

BRIDGE

Bridge is one of our most popular card-games—particularly so among women. It is also one of the most interesting indoor games ever invented, and therefore usually adopted by the hostess who wishes to entertain her
guests for the afternoon or evening.

England greeted the origin of bridge, about fifty years
ago, with great delight. The game speedily became one
of the most popular ones in social circles. Perhaps if
we exclude whist, bridge has taken a greater hold upon
the popular imagination than any other card-game ever
invented.

The origin of the word "bridge" itself is buried in
the mists of uncertainty. Some say that it comes from
the Tartar word "birintch" which means "town-crier."
Others contend that it comes from the Russian word
"biritch" meaning Russian whist. But whatever its origin, the word means a game of such utter interest and
delight, that it should be well understood and frequently
indulged in by hostesses and their guests.

There are two kinds of bridge; one, known as Auction
Bridge is for three players. Ordinary bridge is for four
players. In the former game, one depends largely upon
luck. But skill is a very necessary requisite to the one
who wishes to play and win in ordinary bridge. Writers
on games declare that Auction Bridge is more of a "gambling" game than ordinary bridge. But hostesses who
do not favor "gambling" in any form, had better choose
chess as their popular game, for it is the only game from

GAMES AND SPORT 119

which the element of chance is entirely absent. But bridge, perhaps by virtue of its very element of chance, is to-day one of the most popular indoor games.

The hostess who invites friends to a bridge-party should provide sufficient card tables for the purpose. If the party consists entirely of ladies, it is usually held in the afternoon and light refreshments are served. If men join the party it is usually held in the evening and terminates in a midnight supper.

BILLIARDS AND CROQUET

There seems to be some very intimate connection between croquet and billiards. But while croquet is a very old game and now rapidly lapsing into disuse, billiards is a comparatively new one enjoying very wide popularity. The fact that small billiard tables are being made to fit conveniently into the drawing-room at home, proves that the modern host and hostess recognize the popularity of the game.

Croquet, we find from studying the history of games, was played in the thirteenth century. Billiards, which we speak of as being "comparatively new," was known in the seventeenth century, for does not Shakespeare have Cleopatra say in Antony's temporary absence:

> "Let us to billiards:
> Come, Charmian."

Billiards is a game that lends itself to betting. While this may be permissible in a public billiard place, it is not good form in a private home where the hostess invites a few friends to enjoy the game with her. She should not

120   BOOK OF ETIQUETTE

invite many people unless she has several tables to place at their disposal.

Croquet is played on the lawn. Hidden in the forgotten origin of billiards, there must be some connection between the green lawn of croquet and the green baize cloth of the billiard table. Croquet is played with mallets and balls, very much on the same order as the game of billiards.

The game of croquet is derived from the same source as hockey. The old French word "hoquet," meaning a "crooked stick" has very much the same meaning as the word "croquet." Both are excellent outdoor sports that guests at a house party will find enjoyable and interesting.

One hostess we know, who is a billiard enthusiast, has six tables in her "billiard room," as she calls it, where she entertains several guests almost every afternoon. On the wall is a large picture showing two stately old gentlemen playing a game of billiards, and beneath it in bold hand-lettering, the following bit of verse from Cotton's book, "The Compleat Gamester":

> Billiards from Spain at first derived its name,
> Both an ingenious and a cleanly game.
> One gamester leads (the table green as grass)
> And each like warriors, strive to gain the Pass.

OUTDOOR GAMES

At garden parties, house parties, and lawn parties, there is always the need for interesting, amusing games that will afford entertainment for the guests. The hostess who knows the various games that are popular among the younger and older sets, will be able to spend many

GAMES AND SPORT   121

jolly, pleasant mornings and afternoons with her guests.

Not only for the hostess and her guest, but for every man or woman who loves games and sports, who enjoys being outdoors, there are sports that are as enjoyable as they are health-building. There can be nothing more delightful, on a Saturday afternoon, than to go out on the links and enjoy a good game of golf. And there can be nothing more invigorating to the tired hostess than a brisk game of lawn tennis on a sunny afternoon.

To the splendid outdoor games of America, our young women owe their lithe, graceful bodies and their glowing good health; and our young men owe their well-knit forms and muscular strength. No appeal can be too strong in encouraging people to indulge more freely in outdoor sports—and especially people who spend a great deal of their time in businesses that confine them to offices.

LAWN TENNIS

Tennis is always popular and always interesting.

Those who love the game will enjoy a bit of the history of its origin and of its development in recent years. It is not a new game. The exact date of its origin is not known, and perhaps never will be, but we do know that it was imported into England from France at a very early date. Originally it was called "palmplay" because the palm was used to cast the ball to the other side. And instead of the net, a mud-wall was used to separate the two sides.

The game of tennis flourished in the time of Joan of Arc, for we find her namesake, a certain Jean Margot, born in 1421, called the "amazon of medieval tennis" by Paul Monckton in his book, "Pastimes in Times Past."

122 BOOK OF ETIQUETTE

He tells us also that she could play ball better than any man in France.

In the fifteenth century, tennis fell into disrepute because of the large amount of betting. But gradually, with the passing of the years and the development of the tennis courts, it once more came into its own, and soon we find that it had become so popular and fashionable that it threatened to eclipse even cricket, England's most popular outdoor game. Then once again it lapses into neglect, not to return to the lawns and courts again until 1874. Since that year, Lawn Tennis has steadily risen to the ranks of the most favored social game in America and England. In the past few years changes and improvements have been made and as the game now stands it is truly the "king of games"—as Major Wingfield described it more than two decades ago.

The hostess who invites friends to a tennis game should be sure that her courts are in good condition. It is her duty to supply the net, balls and racquets, although some enthusiasts prefer using their own racquets. Whether or not the hostess joins in the games herself, depends entirely upon her personal preference, and upon convenience. Usually, however, she is expected to play at least one set.

GOLF

The fact that Pepys, in his well-known diary, tells us that he saw the Duke of York playing golf (known then as Paille-Maille) is sufficient evidence of the antiquity of the game. It is of Scotch origin, being played in the Lowlands as early as 1300. The very words "caddie," "links" and "tee" are Scotch. "Caddie" is another word

GAMES AND SPORT

for cad, but the meaning of that word has changed considerably with the passing of the centuries. "Link" means "a bend by the river bank," but literally means a "ridge of land." "Tee" means a "mark on the ground."

It seems that golfing has some strange charm from which there is no escaping once one has experienced it. To play golf and to learn its fascination, is to love it always and be unable to forsake it. James I and Prince Henry his son, were ardent golfers. Charles I was also a lover of golf, and it is related that the news of the Irish Rebellion in 1642 was brought to him while he was playing at the Links at Leith. Sir John Foulis, Earl John of Montrose, Duncan Forbes and the Duke of Hamilton are other notables of history, known to have been addicted to the game.

In 1754 a Golf Club was founded in England, pledging themselves to compete each year for a silver cup. In 1863 another Royal Golf Club was founded of which the Prince of Wales was elected Captain. The minutes and records of this club reveal many interesting, and ofttimes amusing, customs that presaged the very customs practiced by golf-lovers to-day.

One reason why golf is so popular is that it is a sport in which old and young can join on an equal footing. In this manner it is unlike hockey or other similar games, where strength and training are essential. But one must not have the impression that golf can be played once or twice, and then known and understood thoroughly. It is the kind of game that must be played enthusiastically and constantly; and gradually one becomes conscious of a fascination that can hardly be found in any other game or sport.

There is a distinct etiquette of the links that should be

124   BOOK OF ETIQUETTE

known by the hostess who plans a golfing party, and also by everyone who plays the game. Courtesy is one of the unwritten laws of the links. It is considered an unpardonable sin to speak or move when watching another player make a drive. It is also unpardonable to attempt to play through the game of persons who are ahead on the links.

SOME IMPORTANT RULES ABOUT GOLF

In teeing-off, one should be quite sure that one's immediate predecessors from the tee are at least two shots in advance. Otherwise there is danger of injuring other players; and there is also the confusion of driving balls among those of near-by players. If, however, a ball is driven into the space of greensward where another player is concentrating upon his ball an apology should be made.

Sometimes skillful and rapid players find their progress over the links retarded by players who are slow and inaccurate. These slow players may be new at the game, or they may prefer to play slowly. At any rate, it is good form for the rapid players to request that they be permitted to play through ahead of the others; or it is still better for the slow players themselves, when they see that they are retarding others, to volunteer stepping aside while the others play through. A courtesy of this kind requires cordial thanks.

Putting is a delicate and difficult operation upon which the entire success of the game rests. Spectators must keep this in mind when they are on the links, and they must not stand so close to the player that they will interfere with his concentration. It is extremely bad form to talk, whisper or shuffle about while a player is putting,

GAMES AND SPORT 125

and those who do so are revealing their lack of courtesy and of the knowledge of the correct etiquette of sport.

FOOTBALL

We feel that a word about football is necessary, not only because it is one of the most popular American sports, but because men and women alike enjoy watching the game. At the Yale Bowl, where some of the most spectacular football games are played—and won—thousands of men and women from all over the United States gather every year.

Like all other ball games, football is based on many other games that had their origin in medieval times. It was only after the game of kicking the ball had been introduced in England, that it became a distinct sport known as *football*. Since then it has flourished and developed, until to-day it is as popular as tennis, hockey, baseball and golf.

Football is a strenuous game. In England it was confined largely to boys and young men. Even in America elderly men never play the game, but that is no reason why they cannot watch and enjoy it.

There can be no etiquette prescribed for the players in a football game beyond that incorporated in the rules of the game and in the general laws of good sportsmanship. But the people who are watching the game must observe a certain good conduct, if they wish to be considered entirely cultured. For instance, even though the game becomes very exciting, it is bad form to stand up on the seats and shout words of encouragement to the players. Yet how many, who claim to be entirely well-bred, do this very thing!

126 BOOK OF ETIQUETTE

Of course it is permissible to cheer; but it must be remembered that there are correct and incorrect ways of cheering. Noise is noise even in the grandstand, and your loud cheering is very likely to annoy the people around you. A brief hand-clapping is sufficient applause for a good play or even for a victory. It is not necessary to be boisterous. And this holds true of the game of baseball also, when loud cheering serves only to create confusion and disorder.

The well-mannered person is known by his or her calm conduct and gentle manners whether it be in the ballroom or at the football game.

AUTOMOBILE ETIQUETTE

With automobiling enjoying its present universal popularity, it is necessary to add a few paragraphs here regarding the correct automobile etiquette. For there is an etiquette of driving, and a very definite etiquette that must be followed by all who wish to be well-bred.

First there are the rules by which the driver of the car must be governed. In busy city streets, where there are no traffic regulations to govern the reckless driver, one should drive slowly and cautiously. It is time enough to drive speedily when the open roads of the country are reached. But it is inconsiderate and selfish to speed one's car along streets where children are likely to dash unexpectedly in front of the car or where pedestrians are in danger of being thrown down.

A very uncourteous and unkind habit is to sound one's horn wildly, for no other reason than to frighten less fortunate people who have to walk. The horn on the car should be used only to warn people out of the road, or

GAMES AND SPORT 127

when turning a dangerous corner. It should never be used to signal to a person that the car is waiting outside for her.

Care should be exercised in the seating arrangement. The courteous host and hostess take the seats in the center, leaving those on the outside for their guests. If the host is driving, the front seat at his side is a place of honor and should be given to a favored guest.

The people inside the car also have some rules of good conduct to observe. It is bad form to stand up in the car, to sing or shout, or to be in any way boisterous. Automobile parties often speed along country roads shouting at the top of their voices for no other reason than to attract attention—to be noticed. The very first rule of good conduct tells us that this is utterly ill-bred.

It hardly seems necessary to warn the people who are out motoring, not to throw refuse from the car on to the road. Yet we often see paper bags and cigarette boxes hurtling through the air in the wake of some speeding car. This is as bad form as dropping a match-stick on the polished drawing-room floor of one's hostess or home.

AUTOMOBILE PARTIES

Some hostesses plan motor trips for their guests. If it is to be a long trip, requiring an over-night stop at a hotel, the invitations must state clearly, but tactfully, whether they are to be guests throughout the trip, or only while in the motor. Ordinarily, the host and hostess pay all expenses incurred while on the trip.

Gentlemen do not enter the car until the ladies have been comfortably seated. Neither do they smoke in the

BOOK OF ETIQUETTE

car without asking permission to do so. A driver, whether he be the host himself or a hired chauffeur, should be sure that all the guests are comfortably seated before starting. And he should drive slowly to prevent the uncomfortable jolting that usually results when a car is driven at a great speed.

Hostesses often provide linen dusters and goggles for those of their guests who desire them. It is wise, also, to include a few motor blankets, in case the weather changes and the guests become chilly. A considerate host, or hostess, will see that the wind-shield, top and side-curtains are adjusted to the entire comfort of all the occupants of the car.

The dress for an automobile party is a sports suit of some serviceable material that will not show dust readily. The hat should be a small one that will not interfere with the wearer's comfort. In place of a suit one may wear a one-piece dress and a coat but one must never wear light or flimsy materials. If there is to be an overnight stop and one wishes to wear a dinner gown she must have it made of a stuff that will not wrinkle easily or she must be able to make arrangements to have it pressed.

When the car stops and the guests descend, the gentlemen should leave first and help the ladies to descend. If the party stops for refreshments, the chauffeur must not be forgotten. It is a slight that is as unforgivable and discourteous as omitting to serve a guest in one's dining-room. The chauffeur is as much entitled to courtesy as the other members of the party. Of course he does not expect to join the party at their table, nor does he care to eat with the servants of the hotel. The wisest plan is for him to be served in the regular dining-room of the

GAMES AND SPORT 129

hotel, but at another table except when the hotel has special arrangements to meet this condition.

It is always necessary to take the guests on an automobile party back to the place where they started from unless it is distinctly understood from the beginning that some other plan is to be pursued. When planning a motor party consisting of two or more cars, the hostess should be sure to arrange her guests so that only congenial people will be in each car. It is never good form to crowd a car with more people than it can hold comfortably, except in an emergency.

"Careful driving" should be the watchword of everyone who owns a motor. Remember that the streets were not created merely for the owner of the automobile, but for the pedestrian as well.

RIDING

Horse-back riding is one of the favorite outdoor sports of men and women. Which is as it should be, for not only is it excellent for poise and grace, but it is splendid for the health.

A gentleman, when riding with a woman, assists her to mount and dismount. This is true even though a groom accompanies them. In assisting a lady to mount her horse, the gentleman first takes the reins, places them in her hand and then offers his right hand as a step on which to place her foot, unless she prefers to slip her foot in the stirrup and spring up to the saddle unassisted. In this case, it is necessary for him only to hold the horse's head, and to give her the reins when she is comfortably seated in the saddle. He does not mount his own horse until she is mounted and on her way.

130 BOOK OF ETIQUETTE

It is the privilege of the woman rider to set the pace. The gentleman follows at her side or slightly behind. He goes ahead, however, to open gates or lower fences that are too dangerous for her to jump. In dismounting, he again offers his aid, holding her horse and offering his hand if it is necessary to assist her. The lady dismounts on the left side.

At a hunt, a gentleman must sacrifice a great deal of the sport of the chase if there is a woman in the party under his care. He must ride very close to her, taking the easiest way and watching out for her comfort. It is poor form, however, for any woman to follow the hounds in a chase unless she is an accomplished rider. Otherwise she is merely a hindrance to the rest of the party, and especially to the man who is accompanying her.

Be kind to your horse. Do not exhaust it. Do not force it to climb steep hills. Be careful of how you use your spurs. And try to remember that good old proverb, "The best feed of a horse is his master's eye."

Even in the most conservative communities to-day women wear breeches instead of the heavy skirts of a short time back. The cut depends upon the prevailing fashion but the habit should never be of flashing material.

BATHING

The etiquette of the beach has not yet been settled and the chief point of dispute is the way a woman should dress. It is absurd for her to wear a suit that will hamper her movements in the water but it is even worse for her to wear a skimpy garment that makes her the observed of all observers as she parades up and down the beach. There is no set rule as to what kind of suit one should

GAMES AND SPORT 131

wear for one person can wear a thing that makes another ridiculous if not actually vulgar. A well-bred woman is her own best guide and she will no more offend against modesty at the beach than she will in the drawing-room.

SPORTS CLOTHES IN GENERAL

Comfort and style should be attractively combined in sports clothes with the emphasis on comfort. Practicability should never be sacrificed to fashion, and however beautiful they may be to look at, an automobile coat that cannot stand dust, a bathing suit that cannot stand water and a hiking outfit that cannot stand wear are merely ridiculous. There are three questions that the man or woman should first ask themselves before buying a sports outfit. First, Is it comfortable? Next, Is it practical? And last, Is it pleasing?

PART IV

I would rather have a young fellow too much than too little dressed; the excess on that side will wear off, with a little age and reflection; but if he is negligent at twenty, he will be a sloven at forty and intolerable at sixty. Dress yourself fine where others are fine, and plain where others are plain; but take care always that your clothes are well made and fit you, for otherwise they will give you a very awkward air.

—Chesterfield.

CHAPTER I

SPEECH

One is judged first by his dress but this judgment is not final. A better index is his speech. It is said that one can tell during a conversation that lasts not longer than a summer shower whether or not a man is cultivated. Often it does not take even so long, for a raucous tone of voice and grossly ungrammatical or vulgar expressions brand a man at once as beyond the pale of polite society.

No point of social etiquette is quite so valuable as this one of speech. As one goes forth he is weighed in the balance and if he is found wanting here he is quietly dropped by refined and cultured people, and nearly always he is left wondering why with his diamonds and his motors and his money he yet cannot find *entrée* into the inner circles where he would most like to be. Money does not buy everything. If it were possible for it to do so there would be no proverb to the effect that it takes three generations to make a gentleman. And the proverb itself is not more than half true. If the attitude of mind is that of one who honestly wants to develop himself to the highest possible point, mentally, morally, and spiritually, it can be done in much less than a single generation. Of course, much depends upon one's definition of what constitutes a gentleman but for the purpose of this book we mean a man of education, high principles, honor, courtesy, and kindness.

136 BOOK OF ETIQUETTE

CONVERSATION

There is an old Italian proverb that says, "He who has a tongue in his head can go all the world over." But it is not enough merely to have a tongue in one's head. That tongue must have a certain distinct appeal before it becomes the weapon before which all the barriers of social success vanish.

We have all heard the expression, "The magic power of words." Is it a magic power? Or to be more explicit, is conversation an art or a gift? The answer must certainly be an art, for nature never gives that which study accomplishes. And by study you can become a master of speech—you can make words a veritable torch, illuminating you and your surroundings. But words alone mean very little. It is the grouping of words, expressions, phrases; the combination of thoughts that make real conversation.

"In the beginning of the world," said Xanthes, "primitive man was contented to imitate the language of the animals." But as we study the evolution of human nature, we find that man was not long content to imitate the sounds of the animals in the forests. He found the need to express himself, his sensations, his thoughts, in more definite and satisfactory manner. He wanted to share his joys with his neighbors, and he wanted to tell others about his sorrows. And so, nature in her wise judgment, decreed that he should speak, and in his speech should convey his thoughts and ideas to those who listened.

We do not think of these things to-day when we "chatter" aimlessly among ourselves, caring little whether or not we make the most of that wonderful power bestowed

SPEECH

upon us. Yes, speech is a power. It is a most effective weapon, not only to social success, but to the very success of life, if one does not ignore the power of its influence. And that is the purpose of the following paragraphs—to help you realize and profit by the powers of speech and conversation.

THE CHARM OF CORRECT SPEECH

It is strange, but true, that the spirit of conversation is often more important than the ideas expressed. This is especially true in social circles. Since speech is never used in solitude, we may take it for granted that the spoken word is an expression of the longing for human sympathy. Thus, it is a great accomplishment to be able to enter gently and agreeably into the moods and feelings of others, and to cultivate the feelings of sympathy and kindness.

Early in the seventeenth century the *causerie* (chat) was highly esteemed in France. This was a meeting, at the Hotel Rambouillet, of the great nobles, literary people, and intelligent and brilliant women of France, gathered together for the definite purpose of conversation— of "chatting." Among these people, representing the highest intellectual class in France at the time, there developed the taste for daily talks—the tendency of which was toward profound, refined and elegant intercourse according to the standards of that day, and the criticisms offered by the members had a certain influence on the manners and literature of the epoch.

Many years have passed since those days of harmonious gatherings, but we mention them here to draw the comparison between those delightful gatherings of long

138 BOOK OF ETIQUETTE

ago, and our own drawing-rooms and social circles where brilliant men and women gather and converse on topics of immediate interest. If one has imagination, a striking similarity can be noticed between the two.

There is a certain charm in correct speech, a certain beauty in correct conversation. And it is well worth striving for.

COURTESY IN CONVERSATION

A Crow Indian once said to Dr. Lowie, "You Whites show no respect to your sisters. You talk to them." Other instances of how respect and courtesy can be shown in conversation, is found in the traditions and present-day practices of other countries.

In China, for instance, a young man will not introduce into conversation, a topic which has not already been touched upon by his elders. On the Fiji Islands, a woman does not talk to her mother-in-law, and among the Sioux, a young man does not talk at all unless someone else addresses him. These signs of courtesy in conversation have a certain distinct significance in the countries where they are practiced.

Courtesy is the very foundation of all good conversation. Good speech consists as much in listening politely as in talking agreeably. Someone has said, very wisely, "A talker who monopolizes the conversation is by common consent insufferable, and a man who regulates his choice of topics by reference to what interests not his hearers but himself has yet to learn the alphabet of the art." To be agreeable in conversation, one must first learn the law of talking just enough, of listening politely while others speak, and of speaking of that in which one's companions are most interested.

SPEECH

There was a time when bluntness of manner was excused on the ground that the speaker was candid, frank, outspoken. People used to pride themselves upon the fact that in their conversation they had spoken the truth —and hurt some one. To-day there are certain recognized courtesies of speech, and kindliness has taken the place of candidness. There is no longer any excuse for you to say things in your conversation that will cause discomfort or pain to anyone of your hearers.

One should never interrupt unless there is a good reason for it and then it should be done with apologies. It is not courteous to ask a great many questions and personal ones are always taboo. One should be careful not to use over and over and over again the same words and phrases and one should not fall in the habit of asking people to repeat their remarks. Argument should be avoided and contradicting is always discourteous. When it seems that a heated disagreement is about to ensue it is wise tactfully to direct the conversation into other channels as soon as it can be done without too abrupt a turn, for to jerk the talk from one topic to another for the obvious purpose of "switching someone off the track" is in itself very rude.

Let your proverb be, "Talk well, but not too much."

THE VOICE

Ruskin said, "Vulgarity is indicated by coarseness of language." By language he meant not only words and phrases, but coarseness of voice. There can be nothing more characteristic of good breeding than a soft, well-modulated, pleasing voice. This quotation from Demosthenes is only another way of saying it: "As a vessel

140　　**BOOK OF ETIQUETTE**

is known by the sound whether it is cracked or not, so men are proved by their speeches whether they be wise or foolish."

Conversation should be lively without noise. It is not well-bred to be demonstrative in action while speaking, to talk loudly, or to laugh boisterously. Conversation should have less emphasis, and more quietness, more dignified calmness. Some of us are so eager, in our determination to be agreeable in conversation, to dominate the entire room with our voice, that we forget the laws of good conduct. And we wonder why people consider us bores.

Don't be afraid to open your mouth when you talk. First know what you want to say, be sure that it is worth saying, and then say it calmly, confidently, *through your mouth* and not through your nose. Too many people talk through tightly closed teeth and then wonder why people don't understand them. Enunciate clearly and give to your vowels and consonants the proper resonance.

Another mistake to avoid is rapid speaking. To talk slowly and deliberately, is to enhance the pleasure and beauty of the conversation. Rapidity in speech results in indistinctness, and indistinctness leads invariably to monotony.

EASE IN SPEECH

There are two languages of speech—voice and gesture. Voice appeals to the ear, gesture to the eye. It is an agreeable combination of the two that makes conversation pleasant.

"A really well-bred man," a writer once said, "would speak to all kings in the world with as little concern and as much ease as he would speak to you." Confusion is

SPEECH 141

the enemy of eloquence. Self-restraint must be developed before one can hope to be either a good conversationalist or a social success. To create a pleasant, harmonious atmosphere, and at the same time to make one's ideas carry conviction, one must talk with ease and calm assurance.

Try to be naturally courteous and cordial in your speech. It is a mistake to "wear your feelings on your sleeve" and resent everything that everyone else says that does not please you. To become quickly excited, to speak harshly and sarcastically is to sacrifice one's dignity and ease of manner. Know what you want to say, be sure you understand it, and when you say it, be open for criticisms or suggestions from those around you. Do not become flustered and excited merely because someone else does not agree with you. Remember that Homer said, "The tongue speaks wisely when the soul is wise," and surely the soul can be wise only when one is entirely calm, self-confident and at peace with all the world!

LOCAL PHRASES AND MANNERISMS

It is not always easy to drop the local phrases, colloquial expressions and mannerisms to which one has been accustomed for a long time. Yet good society does not tolerate these errors in speech. For they *are* errors, according to the standards of educated men and women.

To use such phrases as "How was that" when you mean "What was that" or "How's things" when you mean "How are you" are provincialisms which have no place in the cultured drawing-room. One must drop *all* bad habits of speech before claiming the "good English which is a passport into good society."

142 BOOK OF ETIQUETTE

Mannerisms in speech are evident in nasal expression and muffled words, spoken through half-closed teeth. We were not meant to speak in that unbeautiful manner, nor were we meant to gesticulate wildly as some of our drawing-room orators persist in doing—to the amusement of everyone else concerned. When you enter the world of good society, drop all your colloquial phrases and mannerisms behind.

IMPORTANCE OF VOCABULARY

Simple expression has the same advantage over flowery language as a simple and artistic room has over a room filled with gaudy, inharmonious embellishments. One is effective, the other defective. And yet to express ideas simply and correctly, with a regard for polish and poise, one must have a good command of the language.

Make a resolve, right now, that you will never use a foreign word when you can give its meaning in English. And also determine now, definitely, that no matter how popular slang becomes in the less refined circles of society, *you* will never use it because you know that it is the badge of vulgarity. There is nothing quite as beautiful as good, simple English, when it is spoken correctly.

To know the right word in the right place, to know its correct pronunciation and spelling, there is nothing more valuable than a good standard dictionary. If you haven't one—a new revised edition—get one right away. You can not hope to become a pleasing conversationalist until you own and use a good dictionary.

An excellent way to increase your vocabulary and perfect your speech is to talk less, and listen politely while others lead the conversation. There's a lot of truth in that old maxim, "Speech is silver, but silence is gold!"

SPEECH   143

INTERRUPTING THE SPEECH OF OTHERS

It was mentioned previously that the Sioux youth does not speak until he is first spoken to. This is also true of the young Armenian woman. She would be horrified at the idea of addressing a woman older than herself, unless first spoken to. Many other countries observe these courtesies of speech, with a wholesome effect upon the general culture of the people.

How often, here in our own country, even in the most highly cultivated society, do we hear a man or woman carelessly interrupt the conversation of another, perhaps an older person, without so much as an apology! It is bad form, to say the least, but it is also distinctly rude. No person of good breeding will interrupt the conversation of another no matter how startling and remarkable an idea he may have. It will be just as startling and remarkable a few minutes later, and the speaker will have gained poise and confidence in the time that he waits for the chance to speak.

Whispering in company is another bad habit that must be avoided. The drawing-room or reception room is no place for personal secrets or hidden bits of gossip. The man or woman commits a serious breach in good conduct by drawing one or two persons aside and whispering something to them.

TACT IN CONVERSATION

Be careful not to give too strong an expression of your likes and dislikes. To master this important point of speech, it is wise to examine carefully and frankly all

BOOK OF ETIQUETTE

your opinions before expressing them in words. It is necessary that you understand yourself, before you are able to make others understand you.

In carrying on a conversation in a public place be sure to keep the voice modulated and do not mention the names of people about whom you are talking in such a way that anyone overhearing the conversation by chance could identify them. It is best to avoid all personal talk when one is in public.

The person who is always trying to set other people right does not use tact. If they wanted assistance, they would probably ask. People are sensitive, and they do not like to have their shortcomings commented upon by others.

Ask questions only if you are gifted with great tact. Otherwise you are bound to create embarrassing situations. If you do ask questions, make them of a general character, rather than personal. But never be curious, because people resent inquisitiveness—and rightly so, for it is a very undesirable trait to have, and each person has a right to privacy.

Never talk for mere talking's sake. Speak only when you have something to say, and then talk quietly, deliberately and with sincerity. Never criticize, antagonize or moralize—and your company will be sought by everyone.

SOME IMPORTANT INFORMATION

If you mumble over your words and have difficulty in pronouncing clearly, you will find it a great help to talk very slowly and take deep breaths between each two or three words. For stammering, deep breathing is also sug-

SPEECH   145

gested before uttering the words upon which one is most
likely to come to grief.

Self-consciousness is the result of exaggerated humil-
ity. If you concentrate upon what you are saying, and
forget all about how you are saying it, you will forget
your shyness. Respect yourself, have confidence in yourself—and nervousness and shyness in conversation will
vanish.

Lisping is a matter of defective speech, and although
reading aloud and dramatic recitations help, it is best
to consult a specialist if ordinary methods fail to prevent it. Such habits as hesitation, coughing, or groping
for a word, are often forms of nervousness and a little
will-power exerted in the right direction may easily control them.

Above all, be simple and be sincere. Let interest in
your subject lend animation to your face and manner.
Do not attempt to make yourself appear brilliant and in-
spired, for you will only succeed in making yourself
ridiculous. Be modest, pleasant, agreeable and sympa-
thetic, and you will find that you win the immediate response of your audience, whether it consists of two people or two hundred people.

WHAT TO TALK ABOUT

In this beautiful country, filled with charming wood-
land scenes, landmarks of interest, museums, schools,
monuments, libraries, there is no excuse for the man or
woman who finds that he or she has "nothing to talk
about." In the newspapers every day, in books, plays,
operas, even in the advertisements and posters, there is
material for interesting conversation.

146   BOOK OF ETIQUETTE

Try it the next time you meet some friends and you find that conversation lags. Talk about something, anything, until you get started. Talk about the sunset you saw last night, or the little crippled boy who was selling newspapers. As long as it is something with a touch of human interest in it, and if you tell it with the desire to please rather than impress, your audience will be interested in your conversation. But to remain quiet, answering only when you are spoken to, and allowing conversation to die each time it reaches you, is a feature of conduct belonging only to the ignorant and dull. There are many pleasant and agreeable things to talk about—argument and discussion have no place in the social drawing-room —and there is no reason why *you* cannot find them and make use of them.

If you are forgetful, and somewhat shy in the company of others, it might be well to jot down and commit to memory any interesting bit of information or news that you feel would be worthy of repetition. It may be an interesting little story, or a clever repartee, or some amusing incident—but whatever it is, make the appeal general. It is a mistake to talk only about those things that interest you; when Matthew Arnold was once asked what his favorite topic for conversation was, he answered, "That in which my companion is most interested."

Make that your ideal, and you can hardly help becoming an agreeable and pleasing conversationalist.

CHAPTER II

DRESS

THE FIRST IMPRESSION

The two most important guides to one's personality are one's appearance and one's manner of speech. Centuries of experience have shown that by means of these one may almost without exception get at least a general idea of the sort of person that lies back of them.

Dress is the most important factor in the first impression. An honest heart may beat beneath the ragged coat, a brilliant intellect may rise above the bright checked suit and the yellow tie, the man in the shabby suit may be a famous writer, the girl in the untidy blouse may be an artist of great promise but as a general rule the chances are against it and such people are dull, flat, stale, and unprofitable both to themselves and to other people.

Like advertising, dress should call attention not to itself but to the person or product which it represents so that people will say, not, "What an attractive gown!" but "What a lovely woman!" not, "What a well-dressed man!" but, "I think I should like to know that man."

There is more room for originality, and by the same token for freakishness in woman's dress, and therefore the greater responsibility is hers. Her clothes should belong to her rather than merely to the era in which she happens to be living. This means that they must be individual but

148 BOOK OF ETIQUETTE

it does not mean that they should be outlandish. Again the golden rule of the Greeks: Moderation in all things.

The attitude of a number of people is expressed in the old limerick:

> As for looks I know I'm no star,
> There are men better looking by far;
> But my face I don't mind it
> For I am behind it.
> It's the folks out in front that I jar.

It is worth while now and then to think of the "folks out in front," and pity for them, if no other feeling, should inspire one to be at all times as well dressed as is within the compass of one's means and ability.

MEN'S DRESS

In the morning when he goes out to business a man should wear a plain serviceable suit of the prevailing cut. If he is invited to an elaborate morning entertainment he may wear the regular cutaway coat and the usual accessories that go along with it. It is always best to follow the local customs with regard to dress and it is absurd for one man to appear at a formal morning affair in the cutaway coat when he knows that all of the other gentlemen present will be in their simple business suits.

For formal afternoon affairs the cutaway is worn while for dinner in the evening full dress is prescribed as it is for any formal entertainment which takes place after six o'clock. To informal garden parties and other similar affairs in the afternoon during the summer, flannels may be worn.

DRESS 149

There are special sporting outfits designed for the man who golfs, plays tennis, rides or motors and the best guide to all of these is a reliable haberdasher. It is his business to keep up with the details of dress and since these are constantly in process of change it is obviously impossible for a book of etiquette to lay down precise rules as to what should be worn.

If a man is to escort a woman he should adapt his costume to hers. If she is to wear evening dress he should also, and if he is in doubt as to whether she is to wear evening dress or a simpler costume, he should ask her. In many cases it rests with the individual which shall be the order of the day.

WOMEN'S DRESS

The woman who goes to business must dress inconspicuously. Clean, freshly laundered white shirt waists with simple dark skirts form the best of outfits. But with laundry bills at prohibitive prices, a substitute must be found for them for the girl in moderate circumstances. For this reason it is more sensible to wear dark serge, silk, or satin fashioned into severely simple frocks relieved perhaps by white linen or organdie collars and cuffs.

The woman who entertains at home in the morning wears a simple frock of the sort in which she may appear on the street. Similarly, in the afternoon unless the occasion is an elaborate one, when she may wear an elegant reception gown or an informal tea, when she may wear one of the exquisite creations especially designed for such occasions.

There is a semi-evening dress which may be worn to afternoon affairs or to dinner and to all evening entertain-

150 BOOK OF ETIQUETTE

ments except very elaborate ones. For these a woman's gown should be *décolleté* and should be of beautiful material. The color and design are at the discretion of the individual but it is well to remember that those which are simplest are most effective.

It is trite to remark that a woman's crowning glory is her hair, but it is true. The manner in which it is arranged should depend upon the kind of costume she is wearing. Only in the evening should she wear heavy bandeaux, aigrettes, etc.

Scattered about elsewhere in these volumes under the theater, etc., more details are given as to the proper kind of dress to wear. Remember this: it is always better to be underdressed than to be overdressed.

THE STORY OF DRESS

It is interesting to note how closely the history of dress parallels the history of civilization. With the awakening of shame came the virtue of modesty. With modesty came the desire for clothes, and clothes brought thoughts of higher ideals, wider desires than those merely of the animal. Out of the desire to cover the body grew the love of decoration, of beauty. Slowly, through the ages, as the love of beauty advanced and was cultivated, an artistic sense developed which is the very flower of our civilization.

Perhaps the most effective way to tell the story of dress is to make this very striking comparison. First let us go back to the time of the prehistoric cave-woman. In her breast the first thought of shame has stirred, and she makes for herself a covering—a dress. She makes it of the skin of a newly killed animal. It is raw and ugly and

DRESS

unpleasant. But the owner feels naught but pride in its ownership, for it is a good skin, impervious alike to the ravages of sun and rain—and its style is exactly like that of the other women in the tribe.

Now let us stand for a moment on a corner of Fifth Avenue, New York's famous avenue of fashion. We see a modern young woman on her way to the theater. From the tips of her French-heeled slippers to the jaunty little hat on her head, she is—perfect. Her gown seems to express in every line the story of her own personality. The color-scheme might well have been invented by Mother Nature herself. The wrap she wears is of sable furs—but how different from the furs of her sister of ancient days! Each skin is exquisitely glossed and dressed, and the whole matched to perfection.

Another young woman passes. She is differently attired in trig tailored suit and smart toque. A business girl. Also perfect. And countless others, streaming endlessly along the wide avenue, men and women, defying in the expression of their own taste and individuality, the decrees of fashion; interpreting silks, cottons, fabrics and furs to harmonize with their own particular personalities, and the story of civilization is told in the clothes they wear.

THE DAWN OF FASHION

It was Cowper who said, "While the world lasts, Fashion will lead it by the nose." And really, hasn't Fashion been a stern monarch throughout the ages? It commanded the Chinese women to have tiny feet—and tiny feet they had to have although it meant months of torture to the young child. It commanded the monstrous

152 BOOK OF ETIQUETTE

ruff of the Elizabethan period, and decreed dignified wigs for the gentlemen of the Colonial days. It decided upon the mantle of the patriarch, the toga of the Roman, the fez of the Turk. Its endless whims and vagaries made the study of dress one of the most curious and fascinating in the world.

How was Fashion created, you ask? To answer thoroughly, we must once more go back to those distant caveman days when dress itself had its inception. At first one simple costume for both men and women distinguished each tribe. There was nothing different in the way the skins were thrown over the body, no embellishments to render any one costume different from those worn by the others. Even at a relatively late date, uniformity of dress among people of one race was like a national characteristic; it was worn by all.

But slowly, as the tiny beam of civilization struggled onward and upward, there came a desire for something more than merely a protection against cold and rain. There came a very intense desire for ornamentation and personal adornment. Thus we find men and women in Central Africa decorating their bodies with stripes of paint, and those who were still more "fashionable" deforming themselves with most weird series of cicatrices on their bodies and faces. In New Guinea we find women who do not indulge in clothing at all, ashamed to appear in public without bracelets on their arms and legs, and ornaments on their heads. So intense did this love of ornament grow among women, that they began to cover their bodies with fur, feathers, shell, beads and countless ornaments. As late as the year 400 the primitive desire for self-adornment is evident. In that year, it is recorded that the wife of the Emperor Honorius died, and when

DRESS

her grave was reopened in 1544, the golden tissues of her shroud were melted and amounted in weight to thirty-six pounds.

Men and women alike hesitated to think for themselves in those earlier periods. Thus, instead of creating "styles" for themselves, they chose the easier method of imitating what others wore—changing it just enough to meet with their own requirements, to satisfy their own undeveloped tastes. One tribe copied what another wore, changing it only slightly according to whim. We find that man soon realized that the accumulation of coverings on his body hindered him in his strenuous activities. It was quite natural, then, that simplicity should dominate his attire, while to woman was left the development of the decorative art.

Fashion was born—and it has remained undisputed ruler ever since.

THE FASHIONS OF TO-DAY

It is not so much in the Fashion of days gone by that we are interested, but in the very delightful fashions of to-day. We all know that the love of beauty is inherent in all women—just as the pride of personal appearance is inherent in all men. It is a heritage brought down through generations of slowly developing culture. And we find to-day that Fashion is the means of expressing individuality.

It would indeed be a Herculean task to attempt to write a discourse on the ever-changing dictates of Fashion, on the constant whims and vagaries of Style. Each season brings forth striking new dress innovations—new colorings, new draperies, new lines. What is in vogue to-day is cast aside to-morrow as "out-of-date."

BOOK OF ETIQUETTE

In the world of good society, dress plays an important part in the expression of culture. There is a proper dress for afternoon wear, and another for evening functions. There are certain costumes for the wedding, and others for the garden fête. The gentleman wears one suit to business, and another to dinner. Where civilization has reached its highest point, there has dress and fashion reached its finest and most exquisite development.

But instinct can be carried to excess. Inherent love of beauty can be so abused that it becomes a sign of vanity. Fashion can be made a series of fads, and style an excuse for eccentricities. It is because men and women, and especially women, are so eager to adopt any new style creation offered to them by the vast army of "authorities," so impatient always for something new, new —that the dress of to-day has earned the censure of students of sociology. "Supply the demand" has ever been the slogan of the producers, while they strive in every way to increase the demand.

And yet, the study of dress is a beautiful one. Women are never so lovely as when they are dressed well. Men are never so attractive as when their garments are faultless. There is something romantic in the gown and veil of the bride, just as there is something delightfully refreshing in the sight of a young girl daintily attired on a hot Summer's day. There is poetry in dress, just as there is in a towering cathedral or in a well-molded statue.

HARMONY IN DRESS

One of the most important, in fact, *the* important principle of dress is harmony. Nature itself is a glorious example of all that is harmonious. Picture, for instance,

DRESS

the delicate pansy, with its soft blend of greens and yellows and purples. Think of the exquisite china-aster with its pale colorings of violet and pink. And the many-hued rainbow that glorifies the sky with a sudden brilliance. How utterly irresistible are these harmonies of Nature, and how well we can all profit by her example!

The spirit of the modern dress seems to be more definitely centered around "sensation" than harmony. We see sport skirts worn with high-heeled shoes, pinks indulged in where navy blue or dark brown would be more appropriate, elaborate motifs and decorations where simplicity should have been. And we see women, priding themselves upon being fashionable, wearing gowns that are pretty enough, but that on them are completely out of harmony.

The reason for this is that so many women, and men too, accept the dictates of Fashion without stopping to determine whether or not these new creations are suitable to their own particular type. They do not realize that to be fashionable does not mean to follow conscientiously every new fad, but to adjust the prevailing style to conform with the lines of their individual faces and forms. To illustrate: it is ridiculous for the very slim young lady to wear a severe straight-line frock simply because it is the fashion, but she can adapt the straight-line effect to her own figure, and add a bit of fluffiness. Similarly, the stout woman need not wear tremendous, voluminous ruffles and flounces because Fashion decrees that they shall be worn, but she may gain the desired effect by using them in moderation.

Why is it that a gown may look thoroughly beautiful on a manikin, but have an entirely different effect when you put it on? Because you have distinct personality,

156 BOOK OF ETIQUETTE

you have little peculiarities of line and coloring that require special consideration. To select lines that harmonize with the lines of your body, colors that harmonize with your own coloring, and styles that harmonize with your particular type, is to dress well and attractively. Seek harmony first—and style afterward.

IMPORTANCE OF COLOR

"White was made for brides," but that is no reason why we, all of us, cannot enjoy it in its cool daintiness, youthful simplicity. White may always be worn—by young and old, at party and dance, in morning and afternoon. It is, and always will be, the ideal color.

But Fashion, in a different mood, demands many hues both soft and brilliant. And here again, whether she dictates pale pink or vivid scarlet, one must be guided by ones own sense of taste and harmony.

The colors of the dress must blend with the natural colors if beauty is to be obtained. Remarkable effects, as startlingly beautiful as the somber afterglow of the setting sun, can be obtained by the correct use of color. It may be contrast or harmony—but there must be a perfect blend.

To illustrate for a few individual types: the sallow-complexioned brunette must never wear yellow, even though it is the favorite color of the season, for it brings out more clearly the yellow lurking in the sallowness of her cheeks. The person with "coal black" hair must avoid blues, light and dark; the colors that most become her are crimson, orange, dark red. Pink is the ideal color for the blond woman with warm coloring; black for the

DRESS 157

woman with fair skin. Pink and green are **for** youth; purple and black are for age. The other colors may be used according to the artistic sense of the wearer.

In selecting material for a gown, the fashionable modiste will first consider the eyes of the lady who is to wear it. Though few but the artist realize it, the eyes are the keynote of the entire costume. They determine whether the dress shall be frivolous or demure, gay or somber, vivid or soft. The color of the hair, also, is important in deciding the color of the gown itself. The soft colors— pink, green, violet, blue—are admirably adapted to blue eyes and light hair while the more brilliant colors are suitable for dark eyes and black hair.

So large a part does color play in the creating of fashions that one must give it correspondingly careful consideration in adapting it to one's complexion and hair. A wrong color has the alarming propensity of marring the beauty of the most charming gown—even as the use of the right color enhances the beauty of the most simple gown. With harmony, style and color the gown needs only the final touch of *personality* to make it perfect. And it is that of which we are now going to speak.

THE CHARM OF PERSONALITY

Dress is an index to character as surely as a table of contents is an index to what a book contains. We know by looking at an over-dressed young person, with a much-beruffled and ornamented frock, that she is vain. We know by glancing at a young man who wears an orange tie, checked hat, and twirls a bamboo cane, that he is inclined to be just the least bit gay. We know by the sim-

158   BOOK OF ETIQUETTE

ple dignity of an elderly woman's dress that she is conservative and well-poised.

In the clothes we wear we reveal to the world the story of our ideals, our principles. If we are frivolous, our clothes show it. If we have a sense of the artistic, our clothes show it. If we are modest, bold, vain or proud the clothes we wear reveal it for all the world to see.

But "Dress changes the manners," Voltaire tells us. It is true; on the stage the "beggar" in his tattered clothes acts and speaks and looks the part of a beggar. At dress rehearsals he plays the part to perfection, but rehearsing in ordinary street clothes he is never quite satisfactory. Something seems to be missing; and that something is personality. The same is true of the rather studious young girl who is also shy and retiring. In her somber clothes, she is perfectly content in the gloomy solitude of her study; but dressed in a filmy little frock of lace and net, with her hair youthfully marcelled, with buckled slippers on her feet, she feels vaguely dissatisfied. She wants to skip and dance and laugh and sing; if she knew psychology and the personality in dress, she would be able to explain it to herself in this manner: clothes so affect the mental outlook, that the wearer unconsciously adopts the personality portrayed.

Can you imagine a Lord Chesterton in tattered clothes, a Queen Elizabeth in a limp calico frock, a George Washington in a conspicuously checked suit? Unmistakable qualities of character are discernible in the clothes we wear—and for that reason we should be particularly careful to make them a true expression of our personality.

Thus when you want to feel light-hearted and free from care, wear delicate fabrics and bright hats. When you want to be thoughtful and solemn, wear heavy clothes

DRESS

and large, drooping hats. Adapt your clothes to your moods, or your moods to your clothes; but have always one ideal in dress—yourself.

This holds equally true of the man. When weighty business matters are to be attended to, dark suits with correspondingly somber ties and shirts attract the desired mood of seriousness. For less sedate, though not less important, occasions, brighter attire makes one forget the cares of business and assume an air of gayety. One may recline in a full-dress suit and strive vainly for rest; but the mere putting on of a smoking jacket brings an immediate feeling of relaxation.

As Haliburton so pointedly said, "As soon as a person begins to dress 'loud' his manners and conversation partake of the same element."

GAUDINESS VERSUS GOOD TASTE

Striking attractiveness, rather than simple good taste, seems to be the spirit of modern dress. To see a beautiful young woman in gaudy clothes is as disappointing as seeing a romantic old Spanish tale bound in a cheap paper cover.

How much more delightful is a simple frock, developed of rich materials, and boasting only deep soft folds of the material as decoration, than an elaborate gown with rows and rows of imitation gold lace! And yet, we find that many of our most fashionable women, priding themselves on having good taste, select clothes that are conspicuous and gaudy rather than those that are simple.

Beauty of material and excellence of workmanship should be the primary considerations in selecting a new gown or suit. If ornament is desired, the laws of har-

BOOK OF ETIQUETTE

mony, contrast and personality should be carefully considered. Colors must blend; there must be no weird contrasts that jar badly on one's artistic sense. Gaudiness, after all, defeats its own purpose, for it expresses a certain vulgarity. The desire to attract attention has no place in the world of good breeding.

Who wishes to be stared at, remarked upon, openly admired—if not the ill-bred woman, the sorely uncultivated man? Good taste finds expression in gowns that are simple, inconspicuous, yet well-cut and artistic; in suits that are quiet, conservative and well-tailored. And the good taste finds its reward in the genuine admiration and keen appreciation of others.

"EXTRAVAGANCE THE GREATEST VULGARITY"

That is what Dr. Crane says—Dr. Crane, who has studied manners in all their aspects. "Extravagance is the greatest vulgarity." How true it is! How many of us adjust the expenditure for clothes in our households, not by what we ourselves can afford, but by what our neighbors and friends spend!

Fashion is a temptress. Smart gowns, exquisite hat creations, attractive styles in bootery, all tempt us to spend more than is really quite necessary. The extravagant woman fills her wardrobe with numerous dresses, blouses and hats for which she has no real use. But how, much more sensible it is to have just enough for one's needs, a few stylish, well-made garments—each one an expression of the wearer's own personality.

There seems to be a false impression among men and women alike, that to be fashionable one must have a new dress for every occasion, a different suit for every day

DRESS 161

of the week. As a matter of fact, this is an entirely mistaken idea. Fashion is not measured by the number of suits or dresses we have, but by the good taste we display in their selection.

It is significant that the woman whose wardrobe is filled to overflowing, invariably finds that she has "nothing to wear," while the woman of taste, with her carefully selected wardrobe, always seems to be dressed just right.

INAPPROPRIATENESS IN CLOTHES

Just as there are certain laws governing the manners and conduct of society, there are certain laws governing the uses of dress. What is correct for the dance, is entirely incorrect for street wear. What one wears on a shopping trip may not be worn to the theater. The gentleman must not wear his business suit to dinner. Occasion governs costume—and its dictates must be heeded if one would be considered both fashionable and well-bred.

There is, for instance, the modish young lady taking an afternoon stroll in high-heeled satin slippers. What could be more inappropriate? Satin slippers should be worn only with semi-evening or evening dress—never with street clothes. Pumps with fur coats are strikingly inconsistent, as are straw hats with winter attire, or velvet hats with dainty summer-time frocks. True fashion does not profess to distort the seasons, although the style authorities would often have us believe so for their own material gain.

Then, of course, there is the young person who is athletically inclined, and insists on wearing sport clothes on all occasions. We see her on a shopping tour, blissfully unaware of how ridiculous her full-pleated skirt and loose

BOOK OF ETIQUETTE

middy appear beneath her elaborate wrap. We see her at a tea, enthusiastic over the glories of the eighteenth hole, and interpreting the glances of her friends at her sport shoes and bright sweater as glances of admiration rather than disapproval. Sport clothes are for the tennis courts, golf links, skating rinks and similar places. They have no place at teas and receptions.

Of the transparent blouses and silk dresses of the business woman, we will speak later; but in drawing a comparison, we might say that they are no more inappropriate than the eccentricities of dress assumed by some of our women of fashion. The importance of this question warrants a special paragraph.

THE ECCENTRIC DRESSER

Many men and women, in the mistaken belief that they are expressing personality, adopt certain peculiarities of dress.

Eccentric dressing always attracts attention, and is therefore bordering on the vulgar. There are, of course, many men and women who enjoy attracting attention, who delight in being considered "different." In such people we are not interested. It is the people of good taste that we wish to advise against the mistake of wearing peculiar and unconventional clothes.

There is a very old tale related about an Egyptian queen who owned a chain of coral, strung on a strip of dried skin from one of their sacred animals. She gloried in the possession of it, and in order to do full justice to it, she forbade everyone in her kingdom to wear beads.

The man or woman of to-day who wears "different" clothes, unconventional and in most cases unbecoming gar-

DRESS 163

ments, is merely obeying the same vain and selfish instinct that prompted that Queen of long ago to forbid the wearing of beads.

As for personality, the man or woman who cannot express it in correct, conservative and conventional clothes, certainly cannot express it in grotesque and eccentric ones.

COMFORT IN CLOTHES

Beautiful dress alone is not enough. We may be attracted to a manikin, but after five minutes or so it bores us. With beauty of dress there must also be a grace and ease of manner without which no man or woman is quite charming, for uncomfortable garments rob us of all poise and grace.

Think of holding a quiet, serious, calm conversation while one's foot aches painfully because of a tight shoe! Think of sitting gravely and patiently through a long concert while one's too-tight collar grows ever more and more irritating, while one's narrow jacket becomes constantly more uncomfortable!

To be uncomfortable is to be conscious of what one is wearing; and we know that well-dressed men and women are never conscious of clothes. They know instinctively that they are well-dressed, and with the knowledge comes a dignity that adds charm to the beauty of their costumes. Thus they are able to enter whole-heartedly into conversation, feeling neither constrained nor uncomfortable but enjoying that serene satisfaction that comes when one is fully aware that one is well-dressed.

The early Romans had two distinct costumes which were worn alike by rich and poor—one simple, flowing

164 BOOK OF ETIQUETTE

garment for the ordinary activities of every-day life, and one that was also simple but a bit more decorative, for the ceremonial occasions. Perhaps the grace and ease of manner for which the Romans of yore were noted was due to the delightful comfort of their dress.

Tight shoes, extreme styles, uncomfortable wraps, coats or suits—anything that in any way makes you conscious of what you are wearing, should be rigidly avoided. You are truly a "slave of fashion" if you allow yourself to suffer hours of torture merely to present an appearance that would have been vastly more pleasing if it had been accompanied by the graceful ease of manner of which discomfort robbed you.

IF ONE IS NOT AVERAGE

We cannot all be perfect "sixteens" or perfect "thirty-sixes." Some of us are taller than others. Some of us are inclined to be stout. Some of us are short, and others very slender. We all have distinct individualities that can be marred or "starred" in the manner of dress we adopt.

We should all study our "good points" and wear the kind of clothes that will emphasize them at the same time that it will conceal our defects. Clothes have the power of magnifying imperfections. The too-stout woman can wear dresses that will make her look twice as stout. The short man can wear suits that make him look very much shorter. Intelligence, good judgment and a sense of beauty will achieve remarkable results for the man or woman who cares about his or her appearance.

There is the very thin woman, for instance. She must avoid the severely straight up-and-down lines that are so appropriate for other women who are built differently.

DRESS 165

Her forte is tunics, large collars, ruffles, overblouses and bows. Soft, filmy materials that fall in graceful lines are especially becoming, as are checked and flowered materials. Stripes in all forms must be strictly avoided as they accentuate the slenderness. For the thin woman, an easy, graceful manner is most important. When she develops such a manner, and combines it with the fluffiest and most frilly of feminine fashions, one will see how very charming she can be.

The too-stout woman faces a more difficult problem. She must carefully consider each detail of her dress, making sure that it does not in any way accentuate her fleshiness. She must avoid the checked and brightly-colored materials that her slender friends may wear. Long lines should be worn, and it should be remembered that clothes without waistlines work wonders for the stout woman— just as the coat without a belt improves the appearance of the stout man. Such edicts of fashion as the tight sleeve, round neck or short waist are not for the stout woman. The ideal dress for her is one long and sweeping in line. The length of the skirt, as well as details of style, must be adapted to her own particular requirements. She will find that she will be much happier (and her friends, too!) if she forgets that she is stout, and does not constantly bewail the fact to those who are with her. It is not deplorable to be stout, but it certainly is deplorable to dress in a manner which emphasizes that stoutness.

TALL AND SHORT PEOPLE

Tall people have a distinct advantage. They are able to wear all styles, all colors, unless they are extremely tall. They seem to have a certain natural grace that lends charm to whatever they wear. But there is the

166   BOOK OF ETIQUETTE

too-tall person who must be careful of what he or she wears. The very tall woman should avoid stripes as they add to her height. She must not wear high collars, nor severely tailored blouses. The tailored suit, however, becomes her. She should avoid bright colors and indulge a great deal in blacks and "midnight" blues. The tall man may wear whatever he pleases—as long as it is not conspicuous. He almost invariably presents an imposing and dignified appearance if he is well dressed.

Short people, especially short women, must exert special care in the selection of their wardrobes. The short woman must select only those gowns that have long lines, long-waisted effects. Bright colors are not for her— except a touch here and there. Short skirts are more becoming than long ones, just as stripes are more becoming than checks. Two extremes that the short woman must never indulge in, are large, drooping hats and extremely high heels. The hat cuts her height, and the heels give her a tilted appearance.

Whether you are tall or short, stout or slender, you have some particular attractiveness, and you should not allow the knowledge of your imperfections to make you timid or awkward. It needs only the correct dress and the proper spirit of pride and dignity to accentuate your personal charms. Remember that it is personality that counts—personality and character—and while some of the world's greatest personalities have been exceptionally tall, just as many of them have been extremely short!

THE WELL-DRESSED WOMAN

Someone once said there is nothing more beautiful than a beautiful woman. A pretty sentiment, but not quite

DRESS

complete. We would have it read: There is nothing more beautiful than a beautiful woman well-dressed.

When is a woman well-dressed? It cannot be when she is merely fashionable, for when we glance at the fading portrait of some forgotten ancestor, graceful in her Colonial gown with its billows and billows of creamy white lace, we feel instinctively that she is well-dressed. And yet, we cannot call her fashionable. It cannot be elaborate attire, for we know that the stylish young miss in her severely tailored suit and sailor hat is certainly well-dressed. It cannot be distinctiveness—or individuality—for many a delightfully well-dressed young woman buys all her frocks and suits in the shops.

No, it is neither of these—and yet, it is all of them. The well-dressed woman has the faculty of charming you —and yet you yourself know not why. You know that she is well-dressed, but when she is gone you cannot remember just what it was that she wore. You have only a faint recollection of a perfect harmony of line and color.

She is fashionable, yes; and elaborate, too, if the occasion warrants it. She is distinctive, but not obviously so. But if she is truly well-dressed, her clothes are of the best materials and the workmanship is faultless. Style, color and line are all incidental to these two dominating principles of dress—material and workmanship.

The striking characteristic of the woman who is well-dressed is her poise, her grace and ease of manner, on all occasions. She is never self-conscious, never uncomfortable. She never is the center of attraction because she is never conspicuous. She is simply yet smartly dressed, graceful yet dignified, attractive yet inconspicuous.

BOOK OF ETIQUETTE

Above all, she is *always* well-dressed—not only on festive occasions.

Every woman has within her the possibilities of being charming—if not beautiful. It requires only the knowledge of correct dress, of harmony and beauty in costume. There is, of course, the woman who insists that she does not care at all about clothes, that she does not care how she is dressed. But she is the exception, and we are interested in the rule. Woman does herself an injustice by being dowdy, careless or commonplace in dress. She puts herself at an unfair disadvantage. Charm and beauty are the heritage of woman, and the world expects it of her.

NOT A SLAVE TO FASHION

The woman who is ruled by fashion may not consider herself a well-dressed woman. If her sense of beauty is developed, if she knows the value of art and harmony, she will not be the slave of a stupid mode. She will not worship at the pedestal of fashion, trembling as each new decree is announced lest she be not among the very first to observe it. Style does not dominate her personality; rather, her personality dominates style.

And after all, is it not absurd to adhere slavishly to that which is in vogue, without attempting to adapt those modes to one's own individuality? There is, for instance, the woman who discards an otherwise attractive and fashionable gown merely because the sleeves are slightly puffed instead of severely tight-fitting as the whim of Fashion demands. She does not stop to consider that puffed sleeves are infinitely more becoming to her. They are not the "latest"—and that fact alone is enough to cause her to discard the gown.

DRESS

An excellent thought for the girl or woman who wishes to be well-dressed, to remember, is: always dress as though you were going to the photographer to have your picture taken—a picture that you are going to leave to your children to remember you by. If you keep this in mind, you will never wear commonplace clothes nor clothes that are extreme in style, but you will dress with simplicity and taste, being sure to add here and there a touch of your very own personality—perhaps a corsage of violets to show your love of flowers, or a rare old cameo brooch to show your reverence for the things grown old.

THE WELL-DRESSED MAN

Few men realize the tremendous importance of clothes both in the social and business worlds. The effects of dress are far-reaching—and they are certainly no less so among men than women.

There is the story of the man who gained admittance to the Athenaeum Library in Boston, although he was not a member. After spending a very pleasant morning reading, he prepared to leave. It was then that he was attracted to a rather dowdy individual who was remonstrating indignantly with an official at the door. "I am a member, I tell you!" he exclaimed. "Well, you certainly don't look it," the other retorted.

The man who had spent a morning in the library hastened away. He had not known that use of the reading rooms was restricted to members. But no one had questioned him, as he *looked* the part of a member. Yet, the man who really did belong, had to submit to the indignity of questioning and of submitting proof, because his appearance—his clothes—did not do justice to his position.

BOOK OF ETIQUETTE

We know that first impressions are the most important, especially in business. The man whose clothes are gaudy, ill-fitting or extreme, will find that he is not making as rapid a stride forward as his abilities warrant. Incorrect dress is a serious handicap. In the social world, it is not only a handicap, but a barrier. The oft-repeated Dutch proverb may be a bit exaggerated, but it certainly has a suggestion of truth—"Clothes Make the Man."

And so we say to the young and the old man alike, dress well. Dress, not as a fashion-plate, but with a regard for appropriate style—and with an especially keen regard for fine materials and excellent workmanship. Do not be content with an ordinary suit, but be sure that each one you wear imparts that poise and dignity which is so essential to the true gentleman. Your wardrobe need not be filled with suits for every day and every occasion; but a few carefully selected garments, well-tailored and smartly styled will earn for you the enviable distinction of "a well-dressed man."

One might remember, to quote once again from the proverbs of the Dutch, that "A smart coat is a good letter of introduction."

THE CHARM OF OLD AGE

Youth may not claim sole possession of charm. Old age has a charm all its own—a silver charm that makes one think of mellowed roses, and fading sunsets.

A delightful gray-and-lilac grandmother, reposing quietly in the depths of a great armchair, perhaps dreaming of a golden youth—this is a picture that artists have long loved to paint. There is something strangely irresistible in old age, especially when old age is beautiful.

DRESS

And to make it beautiful requires only a calm assurance and kind heart combined with clothes that are in good taste and in harmony with one's years and personality.

Of course, one does not expect one's grandmother to wear the same kind of gay creations that young Miss Seventeen delights in; nor would one expect one's grandfather to flaunt the same style of suit one's son wears at college. The sound of rustling silk and sweeping petticoats is one of the charms of the elderly lady—but an abbreviated skirt would certainly make her appear ridiculous. Similarly, the elderly gentleman finds dignity and distinction in a black frock coat, but one is inclined to smile when he appears in the jaunty black-and-white checked Norfolk suit that would better become his son.

Yes, age has a charm that is well worth striving for. There is something decidedly imposing and impressive about a handsome old man immaculately dressed; and there are no words beautiful enough to describe the enchantment of the silver-haired old lady in delicate colors and fabrics, and flowing styles reminiscent of the days of powdered wigs. Old age has its compensations; youth can never have its charming repose and calm.

THE ELDERLY WOMAN

In these days, when daughter and grandmother enjoy the same entertainments, and attend the same affairs, the clothes of the elderly woman are just as important as those of the younger. We shall describe here several kinds of costumes that invariably add charm to old age, so that grandmother may appear to advantage beside the youthful bloom of the young girl.

There is, for instance, the soft, wide lace fichu so be-

172   BOOK OF ETIQUETTE

coming to the elderly woman—but that the young miss cannot very well wear. Combined with a dress of brocaded satin, with a full skirt that takes one back to the days of the Quakers, the lace fichu is most attractive. Then there is always the shadowy charm of black velvet and black lace. For the more formal occasions when the elderly woman wishes to be particularly well-dressed, yet not conspicuous, a dress of black velvet, with wide frills of black Chantilly lace, makes a most appropriate costume. The lace may be used to veil the skirt and as sleeves.

The elderly woman may choose any dark color that becomes her—gray, dark blue and black are perhaps the three colors most favored. There are several light colors that are appropriate, chief among them, gray and lavendar. Materials worn by the woman-who-is-older are taffeta, velvet, *crêpe de chine* and satin. She should avoid such materials as organdie, georgette and tulle—they are meant for youth.

IMITATION AND OVER-DRESSING

Two of the most common faults of elderly women are imitation and over-dressing. Both rob old age of its charm, and the wise woman will conscientiously avoid them.

By imitation, we mean the following of fashions and styles meant for the young person. We see women celebrating their fiftieth wedding anniversaries wearing "fashionable" dresses that are in absolute discord with their years and personality. Short skirts and straight-line silhouettes may be perfectly all right, but they certainly do not give to old age the imposing dignity that is its main charm.

DRESS 173

One instinctively respects and admires the white-haired woman whose skirts are of a length commensurate with her age and dignity, and who carries herself with calm poise. More than that, one *appreciates* her. But the woman who is growing old and insists upon keeping herself young by wearing inappropriate and inharmonious clothes, is merely making a farce of herself. There can be nothing more ridiculous than a woman past fifty in gown and wrap obviously created for the young person of seventeen. Instead of improving her appearance, the the elderly woman deprives herself of the charm that should rightfully be hers.

As for over-dressing, it is so utterly bad form and bad taste that it requires only passing notice. Just as simplicity enhances the beauty of youth, so does simplicity enhance the charm of old-age. Ostentation of any kind, jewels, bright colors, gaudy styles—all these make old age awkward, unpresentable and unrefined.

THE OLDER GENTLEMAN

One can be a good many years past fifty and still enjoy the theater, the opera. And one can easily retain the presentable dignity of earlier days by wearing clothes that are just as appropriate as those of those earlier days.

For afternoon wear the elderly man will find the black frock coat with gray trousers most effective. He should wear white linen, wing collar and small black tie. This costume is also appropriate for morning wear. In the evening the gentleman always wears full dress, irrespective of age.

In the warmer climates, gentlemen of more mature

174 BOOK OF ETIQUETTE

years find keen pleasure in the early morning and afternoon costume consisting of black and white patterned
homespun jacket, slacks and waistcoat of white flannel,
white linen and foulard tie. Black and white sport shoes
and a light panama hat complete the costume admirably.

A TRIP TO THE SOUTH

Because it is the trip about which people are most in
doubt when it comes to deciding what to take along we
give here below a few suggestions about the wardrobe for
a person about to start South.

To visit the balmy sunshine of the South, is to require
a wardrobe that will harmonize with the lazy mood of
the skies of Havana or Miami. Even though the snows
may have tied up traffic in one's own home town, clothes
for the Southland trip must be delicate, "summery" and
flimsy. One includes a bathing suit, too, although the
lake back home is frozen over.

The wardrobe one takes to the South depends largely
upon the duration of the visit and the extent of one's
purse. The one described here is for the average requirements of both.

For the mornings there must be several crisp, demure
little frocks that are easy to launder. Bright colors
match bright skies, and wide sashes are most becoming.
For afternoon wear, frocks of taffeta, silk and organdie
are suggested—colorful little frocks made with a regard
for easy packing and attractiveness. Canton crêpe is a
lovely material, especially when it is of pale apricot or
Nile green—and it does not crush as easily as taffeta or
organdie. A delightful frock for Southern wear is hand-

DRESS   175

sewn voile in a soft old rose shade. With it may be worn
a large-brimmed straw hat of old rose.

Bright sweaters, sport skirts, sport coats, blouses, oxfords—all these are of course indispensable to the wardrobe for the southern visit. The number of sweaters and
blouses taken depends upon the length of the visit. One
should include a bathing suit, a beach coat and a brightly-
colored parasol. And the smart frock for evening strolls
must not be forgotten.

At least one elaborate evening gown, and two or three
semi-evening gowns will be necessary even if the visit to
the South is a short one. And we would heartily recom-
mend a fluffy little evening wrap to go with the gown.
Then, of course, there are the little strapped slippers and
the low-cut sports shoes to be considered.

One is pretty sure to be happy under the blue skies of
the tropics if one's wardrobe contains a plentiful supply
of gay, colorful frocks, blouses and sports things. But
one need not postpone the visit because clothes seem to be
expensive; common sense, good judgment and a small
purse go a long way.

FOR THE GENTLEMAN

Plenty of white duck trousers, white linen, light sack
coats and sports clothes are necessary for the man who
winters in the South. He will find the patterned homespun jacket very smart indeed, with slacks and waistcoat
of white flannel. This outfit may be worn with panama
hat, colored foulard tie and black and white sports shoes.

A brown or gray flannel sack suit is convenient for
Southern wear—especially in the morning and early afternoon. It is attractive when worn with tan oxfords, colored

176 BOOK OF ETIQUETTE

linen and straw hat. Flannel suits are often worn with white oxfords, and sometimes blue serge sack jackets with white duck trousers.

The wise man will include a suit for motoring in his wardrobe. With it he should include a motor cap, and a light raglan coat or a coat of unshorn homespun. An attractive tennis jacket for Southern wear is of blue and black striped English flannel, with a wide roll collar; worn with white linen and white flannel trousers. White tennis shoes should be included for wear with this outfit.

For the afternoon, an attractive costume for the gentleman in the South is a single-breasted jacket of diamond weave homespun, a double-breasted vest to match, white flannel trousers and white linen. A black tie with polka dots of white, and black and white sports shoes add just the right note of smartness.

A dinner jacket and full dress suit must have place in the wardrobe one prepares for the South. Patent leather pumps should not be forgotten, nor a silk hat for the very formal occasions. Of course, there must be plenty of white and colored linen, and a generous supply of bright ties and sports shoes and hose. As for bathing suit, golf togs and riding habits, we leave these to the taste and discrimination of the gentleman who is contemplating the visit.

CHAPTER III

THE BUSINESS WOMAN

WOMAN IN THE BUSINESS WORLD

There was a time, not so very long ago, when woman's activities were confined to the home. For a woman to be actively engaged in some business or profession of her own meant one of two things: either she was an "old maid" or she was "queer." Naturally, the social standing of such women was rather doubtful.

But to-day, with the equal franchise that has given woman her long-denied vote, she has allowed her talents and capabilities to find outlet in other wider fields than those limited merely to the home. There are women in law offices, women in courts as reporters and interpreters, women in the stock exchange, women editors, women directors—women in every conceivable branch of art, industry and commerce. That they are succeeding, admirably so, is evident in their social status.

Years of blind adherence to false tradition have robbed woman of her proper development along business lines. That explains why there is still a difference in the business status of men and women. Then, of course, there is the sex difference; and advanced though she prides herself on being, woman is still considered mentally inferior— for the simple reason that she *is* a woman. It may take many years of slow development before woman is con-

177

178 BOOK OF ETIQUETTE

sidered man's absolute equal—in business as in politics. And until that time arrives, it behooves every woman who is interested in the progress of womanhood, to do her little share in hastening that glorious time of complete equality.

One of the seemingly small, but really vital things woman can do, is to dress so well and so wisely in business that the most exacting man can find no excuse to condemn her as a "slave of fashion."

SELF-CONFIDENCE

Poise, self-confidence, dignity—all these come with the knowledge that one is well-dressed. The business woman cannot afford to sacrifice self-confidence, if she wishes to make a success. Self-confidence brings with it a certain forcefulness of manner, a certain dignity of bearing that is convincing at the same time that it is impressive.

And clothes play a large part in the development of this self-confidence! Yes, clothes, for it is when one knows and feels instinctively that one is perfectly attired, yet inconspicuous, that one is in full command of one's thoughts and bearing. The woman who would be a success in business, must remember that she cannot do justice to the business of the moment, if she is wondering whether her skirt falls just right, whether her blouse is still crisply laundered, whether the colors she is wearing are not too bright. She becomes embarrassed, flustered—and she fails to do justice to whatever should have been claiming her attention.

Recently, we read in the newspapers about a woman lawyer defending a young man accused of murder. We read with a great deal of interest, that she was a com-

THE BUSINESS WOMAN 179

paratively young woman, and inclined to be eloquent in her speech. We read parts of her rebuttals to the court, and we tried to picture her standing in the center of the huge room, surrounded by eager spectators, facing the jury,—in a gown that was fashionable, becoming, yet inappropriate and uncomfortable. We could not do it. We *knew* that she could never have made the impassioned appeal that freed the defendant if she had been thinking of her clothes, rather than of the case. We pictured her in a conservative suit, with high-necked waist, strictly tailored throughout, and giving the appearance of being well-dressed without anyone even stopping to think about it. Later we were gratified to learn definitely that we were correct—this woman lawyer who had made so tremendous a success was an extremely conservative dresser, with simple good taste.

Self-confidence, poise and dignity are valuable assets to have in business. Correct dress aids materially in their development.

THE SLATTERN

It hardly seems necessary in a book of this kind to speak about the slattern. And yet, some bits of advice we can give may be of value to some—and therefore we will not omit them.

By a slattern we mean a woman who shows lack of care and thought in clothing. The girl whose blouse sags is a slattern. The woman whose dress hangs loosely and does not fit well is a slattern. The woman who looks as though she had jumped into her clothes quickly, dashed off to the office without glancing in the mirror, and then forgotten

180 BOOK OF ETIQUETTE

all about straightening her hat and belt, is a slattern. Broadly speaking, any woman is a slattern who is not scrupulously careful in her attire, who does not show by her very appearance that she is well-groomed, well cared for.

One can be perfectly groomed with the possession of just one suit. A girl who is planning to have an illustrious career, and who wishes to put aside her earnings with a view towards future investments, need not spend large sums on clothes. With one very smart, tailored suit of a good material, and several attractive blouses, she can always look neat and well-dressed. Satin blouses, tucked and high-necked, are excellent for the office. A soft, fluffy little blouse of georgette transforms the suit into a quite appropriate costume for visiting and entertaining.

There can be no excuse for the girl or woman who does not always look her best at business as well as when she is attending to her social duties. And being well-dressed does not mean expensively or elaborately dressed. Some of the best groomed women wear clothes that are striking because of their very simplicity.

FOLLOWING THE FASHIONS

Changing constantly as they do, Fashions must be followed wisely. To adopt each new style as it is presented, stopping to question neither its authenticity nor permanency, is to become very soon a literal "slave of fashion." To avoid this, women of good taste adopt only those new fashions that are conservative and not obviously "new." Anything radically different, anything extreme, should be strictly avoided.

The business woman should pay particular attention to

THE BUSINESS WOMAN 181

the selecting of styles for her dresses, blouses and suits. She should never select a dress that is made with some distinct feature that may be worn for a month or two and then discarded. She should never search among the "fads" for her blouses, but choose instead those simple, tailored, becoming waists that are so appropriate for business. Her suits should always be dark in color, of excellent material, and of a style that is amply conservative enough to be worn two seasons if necessary.

If fashions are chosen wisely, with a regard for simplicity; if, in fact, clothes are chosen for good cut and fine material rather than attractive style, the business woman will soon find that she is gaining a reputation for being at all times well-dressed. And it is a reputation she will find valuable.

GAUDY ATTRACTION

One need only step into a modern office for a moment, and glance around at the stenographers in their thin georgette blouses and high-heeled shoes, to realize how inappropriate gaudy, attractive clothes are in the business atmosphere. The stenographers may continue to wear their flimsy waists and gaudy clothes without ever feeling sorry for it, but the business person who expects to have a worthy career, will find ostentation in clothes, and especially gaudy display, fatally detrimental to her ultimate success.

There is nothing more conducive to respect, trust and honor in business than quiet tastes—in clothes as in everything else. One instinctively respects the young lady who is smartly attired in dark, simple clothes, ideally adapted to the business environment. How much more

BOOK OF ETIQUETTE

sensible she looks, how much more eager one is to trust her with confidential information, with responsible duties, than the flippant person who wears gaudy clothes! The wise woman will never allow bad taste to influence her to wear bright, attractive things to business; what she lacks in good taste and the knowledge of correct dress, she will make up in good common sense.

Someone once said, "There must be a reason for everything." There must be, then, a good reason for everything we wear. And surely there can be no reason for a bright orange georgette waist, or a finely plaited white *crêpe de chine* skirt worn to business. Women who wish to succeed in business, should avoid all that is gaudy, useless and inappropriate in dress, wearing only what is simple, becoming and neat.

THE BUSINESS SUIT

The correctly-tailored, neat business suit is indispensable—as any business woman will attest. There seems to be a dignity about a suit that is lacking in any other business garment. Perhaps it is because of its simplicity.

For the woman who wishes to be tailored, we suggest the smart English tweed suits that are always in good taste. They may be simple, belted models with large patch pockets and straight-line jackets. Heather is a good color, or gray or brown mixture. Worn with plain white lawn or white batiste blouses, suits of this kind are ideal for business wear.

Jersey suits are also appropriate, if they are developed in dark colors, and simple styles. Loose, belted jackets are always in style, or they may be slightly fitted at the waist. Most popular and most becoming of all is the navy

THE BUSINESS WOMAN 183

blue serge suit. It is always appropriate. It can be worn with white or colored blouses, and always presents a neat appearance. If it is well made and fits perfectly it will impart that well-groomed look so important to business women. For exact style of suit, fashion magazines or personal tailors must be consulted.

In the summer a woman may with propriety wear simple frocks of gingham, chambray, linen, and other washable materials.

THE BUSINESS DRESS AND COAT

Dark colors and heavy materials are always better form for business frocks than light, colorful materials. Good taste is undeniably evident in the simple, one-piece business dress of navy blue serge or tricotine. A bit of lace at the neck, or perhaps some touch of bright color, relieves the sombre darkness of the dress yet does not add any undue or inappropriate attraction.

Please remember we are not trying to preach here, or lecture you on the extremes of style. What we are attempting to do is merely point out for you what is correct and incorrect to wear in business circles, and we feel sure that you can make no mistake by following our advice.

For instance, there is the woman who is seeking valiantly to make a success in some line of business hitherto barred to women. Yet she wears an expensive fur coat and attractive frocks that would be better fitted to the dance floor. She wonders why her superiors hesitate to trust her with important responsibilities. She does not realize that her lack of discrimination in dress, her evident lack of knowledge of what is correct to wear at business, has caused them to lose confidence in her.

184 BOOK OF ETIQUETTE

The business coat should be of cloth, never completely of fur unless one's position is high enough to warrant it—and even then it should be only of one fur, instead of a combination of two or three, and made with a regard for simplicity and inconspicuousness. However, the most appropriate business coat is made of a heavy cloth, plain or fur-trimmed for winter, and light-weight, dark-colored material for the warmer days. The hat, of course, follows the general note of simplicity and is usually small and dark. A turban is excellent, and it is one of the few fashions in hats that remains always popular.

AN APPEAL TO BUSINESS WOMEN

It took many centuries of hammering before the portals of business and industry and art were thrown wide open to women. Now that that has happened it is her duty and pride to conduct herself in such a way that there can be no regrets and vain longings for the return of the woman of yesterday. By her manner and her dress a woman determines her place, and the women who are careless of their appearance and careless of their standard are the ones who are hindering the progress of women toward the goal of perfect womanhood.

When she enters business she must realize that she is on an equal footing with men and she should not demand or expect privileges simply because she is a woman. What she does and says and wears during the hours of her social life is entirely distinct from her business life, though, of course, she is always courteous, however hard it may be sometimes to control herself under the grinding of the routine work at the office.

CHAPTER IV

ON THE STREET

THE TRUE ETIQUETTE

Etiquette, in its truest sense, is an exponent of *self*, rather than a manifestation towards *others*. We do what is right and courteous because no other behavior possibly could be consistent with our claim to be well-bred.

As Shakespeare has said,

"To thine own self be true;
And it must follow as the night the day,
Thou canst not then be false to any man."

Instinctively, and with no thought of impressing others, the well-bred man does and says what is correct. And his manners are as polished and cultivated in his home, at business and in public, as they are at the most formal social functions.

It is not enough to observe the conventions of society when you are in the elaborate ballroom or at a fashionable dinner. You must be always, at all times, in all places, as courteous and well-mannered as you would be in the most impressive surroundings. The world judges you by your manners in the street car and on the avenue just as severely as it does in private homes and at social functions.

Do what is correct because you are well-bred, and not because some important person is watching you. Then you will truly be following the rules of courtesy.

186   BOOK OF ETIQUETTE

POISE IN PUBLIC

"Mightiest powers by deepest calms are fed" says the
proverb. And Dr. Crane, himself a mighty power, supple-
ments the saying by one of his own—"The silent sun is
mightier than the whirlwind."

It is the quiet well-mannered person who inspires respect
and liking. The loud laugh bespeaks the vacant mind and
noisy, boisterous conduct has a tendency to irritate and
make nervous the people who have to come into contact
with it. In public and elsewhere you are accredited with as
much refinement and gentility as your manners display—
no more.

It is a mark of extreme good breeding to be able to meet
all emergencies calmly and without uncontrolled anger or
excitement. In training in the etiquette of calm behavior,
there can be no better test than that of controlling the
temper. Do not confuse this serenity of manner with
cowardice; for the calm dignity that forbids one to be ill-
mannered also forbids one to endure insolence. By learning to control the temper, one develops that kind of poise
which is undeniably one of the greatest assets in the social
and business worlds.

THE CHARM OF COURTESY

Real culture has a tendency to avoid excessive individuality. Instead, it requires that all people be treated with
equal courtesy, whether they are strangers in the street
of friends in the drawing-room. And it is this very charm
of courtesy that has made etiquette so important a factor
in civilization.

ON THE STREET 187

"All doors open to courtesy," the proverbs tell us. The "general public" so sadly abused in book and speech, is quick to recognize courtesy and eager to respond to it. Before a pleasant face and a courteous manner, all obstacles vanish, and we find ourselves progressing easily through the world, making friends as we go.

Some of us vainly pride ourselves upon being frank and candid in our association with others. This is a serious blunder which many men and women make. It is not commendable to be frank, when courtesy is sacrificed. Be truthful and just, but do not be unkind. And it certainly is unkind to repeat bits of gossip or scandal, unless there is a special reason why it should be done. How much better it is to gain the reputation of being considerate than the reputation of being brutally frank!

There are countless trifling tests of good manners that distinguish the well-bred. And these same tests prove that a careful attention to the rights and comforts of others, is one of the most decided marks of good breeding. For instance, at the postoffice one can immediately discern the well-bred man. He stands quietly in line until there is room for him at the window. He does not crowd. He does not attempt to push ahead of others to reach the window before his turn. He does not interfere with other people's business; he would be horrified at the thought of deliberately loitering near a window to overhear the private affairs of some other man. He is quiet, unobtrusive and considerate, moving quickly away from the window for the next person's convenience. In manner and speech, he is essentially *courteous*.

It is impossible to be a lady or gentleman without *gentle* manners. And it is impossible to have gentle manners without being *courteous*. The word "courtesy" to-day

188   BOOK OF ETIQUETTE

should carry the same meaning of beauty and charm that
the word "chivalry" did in the eighteenth and nineteenth
centuries.

LADIES AND GENTLEMEN

There was a time, not so long ago, when a most marked
reserve was required between men and women in public.
But to-day, with the advent of women into almost every
branch of business, art and profession, there is a tendency
to loosen this social barrier and create a more friendly
relationship between men and women. The stiff formali-
ties of a decade ago have given way to a much more pleasing social harmony and understanding.

"Etiquette requires that the association of men and
women in refined circles shall be frank without freedom,
friendly without familiarity" declares a recent writer on
good manners. There is no longer need for the strained
reserve formerly felt when women were in the company of
men in public. If the correct rules of etiquette are observed, and courtesy and poise follow in their wake, the
man and woman in public may be as entirely at ease and
unrestrained as they would be in a drawing-room or at an
informal dinner.

American gentlemen have the reputation of being more
chivalrous than the gentlemen of any other country.
American ladies are acclaimed the most charming and intelligent in the world. Thus, when the speaker on the
platform addresses the public audience as "Ladies and
Gentlemen" the expression should mean something more
than merely a careless formality.

WHEN TO BOW IN PUBLIC

To bow or not to bow is often a puzzling question!

ON THE STREET 189

Some authorities on etiquette claim that "it is correct to bow first to a person of higher social position." Others assert that social position has nothing to do with it, and that it is age alone that determines who shall bow first. The question devolves upon several very important rules that should be rigidly observed.

The first, and invariable rule, is that the woman always bows first when meeting men acquaintances. Her bow assumes the proportions of a simple greeting; the head is slightly inclined, she looks directly at the man recognized, and smiles cordially. To the woman, therefore, is given the privilege of recognizing or refusing to recognize a man acquaintance. However, the really well-bred woman will never ignore in public a person, man or woman, with whom she has had even a slight acquaintance—unless she has a very good reason to do so.

Two young women meeting in public greet each other with a certain degree of spontaneity which consequently eliminates any question regarding the first bow. But when one of the women is married and the other unmarried, the first bow invariably comes from the former. Younger people, of the same sex, always wait for the first sign of recognition from the older person.

Young women who are dance partners or partners at the dinner table with men who are not personal friends, incur the social obligation of bowing courteously when chance meetings are made in public, even though there is no desire to continue social acquaintanceship. Also, when a man or woman has been invited to an entertainment at a house through the good offices of a friend of the hostess, he or she must wait to receive first recognition from that hostess when meeting in public.

190 BOOK OF ETIQUETTE

Gentlemen meeting each other in public observe the same rule as that outlined for two women,—the younger waits for first recognition from the elder. If both are of the same age, the question of first bow is unimportant. People meeting often during the day need not bow elaborately each time; a simple smile or glance of recognition is sufficient.

It is extremely rude and unkind to "cut" an acquaintance publicly by staring coldly in response to a courteous bow and smile. There are so many more dignified methods of terminating an undesirable acquaintanceship. It is necessary only to keep one's eyes averted, persistently but not obviously if one wishes to avoid greeting an undesirable acquaintance. Or if one wishes one may bow with extreme formality, but a bow and smile in public should always receive some kind of acknowledgement, no matter how severely formal.

WALKING IN PUBLIC

First in importance to remember when walking in public is poise and balance of bearing. The expression "the *débutante's* slouch" is a direct result of the lazy manner of walking recently adopted by a number of young women. Aside from its bad effect upon health, this manner of walking is both ungraceful and unattractive. Men and women both should remember that an erect, well-poised bearing is more impressive than the most elaborate costume.

A lady does not take a gentleman's arm when walking with him in the daytime unless she is elderly or infirm. It is only after dark that she properly accepts the support of her escort. In this case, she merely rests the palm of her hand lightly within the curve of his elbow. It is extremely bad form, as well as ungraceful, for her to link her

ON THE STREET 191

arm through his. The gentleman always walks nearest the curb unless on a special occasion when the street is very crowded and he wishes to protect her from the jostling crowds. He may offer his arm to the lady in crossing dangerous streets or to guide her through congested traffic.

When walking with two ladies, a gentleman's proper position is not between them; if it is in the evening, he offers his arm to the elder lady and the other friend walks by her side. There seems to be a mistaken belief that a gentleman walking with two ladies must "sandwich" himself between them, but correct social usage teaches that this is entirely wrong. The ladies always walk side by side.

On no occasion may a gentleman take a woman's arm. Good society regards this as a disrespectful freedom. Thus, whenever he feels that she needs his protection, a gentleman should offer a lady his arm, but never attempt to thrust his hand through her arm. It is not even correct for him to grasp her by the elbow (as so many young men insist upon doing!) when crossing a street.

STOPPING FOR A CHAT

Very often we meet, in the course of our daily strolls, old friends or acquaintances with whom we are eager to have a little chat. This is entirely permissible, if certain laws of good conduct are observed. One should never stop on the street to talk, but should walk on slowly with the person with whom one wishes to converse.

Remember that primarily all conduct in public should be characterized by reserve. While it is entirely allowable to call a jolly "Hello!" to a friend one meets in a country lane, even though one still is fifty rods away, it would be

192 BOOK OF ETIQUETTE

extremely bad form on Broadway or Fifth Avenue—or
Main Street in any town. A cordial but quiet greeting
shows good breeding; a greeting so conspicuous that it
attracts attention is never in good form.

Conversation should be carried on in quiet and subdued
tones. Above all, be natural in your speech. Do not attempt to be flowery in your language, or "different"
merely because there are strangers around to hear—and
admire. And if you do stop to converse with your old
friend, be sure that you speak sensibly of things of mutual
interest; there is no excuse to stop merely for the sake of
exchanging inanities.

Whispering is as rude in public as it is in the ballroom
or at the dinner table. Confidential business should not
be discussed on the street or in the department store; the
proper place for such private affairs is in the office or
parlor.

If addressed by a stranger seeking information regarding a certain street or number, show a cheerful and kindly
interest. It is perplexing and often embarrassing to be
in an unfamiliar town or country, and whatever information you give should be in an interested and courteous
manner.

Someone once said, "If you must do a thing, do it with
all your heart. To do it half-heartedly is to rob it of all
its charm." Let this be your motto in regard to the
courtesy extended strangers who seek your aid.

WHEN ACCIDENTS HAPPEN

Gibbon said, "Accident is commonly the parent of disorder." But where there are only people of culture and
fine breeding, an accident is devoid of all haste, hysteria

ON THE STREET 193

or other indications of disorder of any kind. It is the final test of correct manners, this being able to conduct oneself with calmness and dignity even in moments of most distracting circumstances. And besides its cultural aspects, calmness in time of danger or accident is often the means of saving lives.

The rules of good breeding are nothing more than the rules of good sense and these are never put to a more severe test than when an accident occurs. The person who can keep his head during a fire will be much more likely to get out of the building than one who loses all control of himself and becomes hysterical. Presence of mind when someone faints or is hurt or is in danger often prevents a serious or fatal mishap and always eliminates a large part of the disorder incidental to such occasions.

When an automobile or railroad disaster occurs, it is the calm person who is most helpful. And surely helpfulness is one of the basic terms of good conduct everywhere.

ACCEPTING COURTESIES FROM STRANGERS

Ella Wheeler Wilcox, writing about etiquette, said "Etiquette is another name for kind thought. The man who says 'I know nothing about etiquette' does not realize that he is saying 'I know nothing about courtesy to my fellow beings.'" One of the reasons why America has truly been the land of golden promise to so many strangers from other shores, is that there are always so many men and women eager to help, eager to show those little courtesies that warm the heart and rekindle the dying spirit. Etiquette and courtesy are synonymous.

But it is not alone with the giving of courtesies that we are interested. It is important that we know the correct

194   **BOOK OF ETIQUETTE**

way to accept them. And it is particularly important that we know the correct way to accept courtesies extended to us in public. There can be nothing more discouraging to the lover of social etiquette than to see a man give up his seat in the car to a woman who accepts it without a word of thanks or a smile.

The question has often been asked whether or not it is correct for a woman to accept the offer of shelter of an umbrella offered her by a gentleman who is a perfect stranger. To settle this definitely, we say that it is absolutely bad form for a woman to accept this courtesy no matter how hard it is raining and how important the need of saving her clothes may be. She may, however, accept the courtesy if it is offered by a gentleman to whom she has been introduced at a dinner, dance, theater party, or other social function.

If a woman drops her bag or gloves and they are retrieved by a passing man, it is necessary only to smile and say "Thank you." No further conversation is permissible. But if a man saves her from some grave danger, such as being thrown down by a horse, or run over by a car, it is not only necessary for her to thank him but the woman should ask, "May I have the pleasure of knowing to whom I am indebted?" To offer further expression of her obligation the woman would later send some male member of her family, a brother or husband, to the home of the man who has been of service to her. She should never offer money in appreciation of the service, unless it is evident that he is a working man; and even then she should use tact.

Such courtesies as assisting to pick up bundles that have dropped to the ground, opening a door that has stuck or giving desired information, require only the conventional "Thank you." No courtesy, however slight, should

ON THE STREET 195

be accepted without evidence of gratification, even though it be but a slight smile.

RAISING THE HAT

When bowing to a woman or in acknowledgment of a greeting, when walking with a woman and bowing to another man of his acquaintance, a gentleman raises his hat. Similarly, when bowing to a man who is accompanied by a woman, the courtesy is observed and also when a man is walking with another man who lifts his hat in greetings to a friend, whether or not that friend is known to him personally. The hat is also raised whenever a gentleman offers a civility to a lady, whether she be friend or stranger.

Elderly men, superiors in office, clergymen and men of distinction are entitled to the courtesy of lifting the hat. "Hat in hand goes through the land" say the Germans. And "Cap in hand never did any harm" is the gem we find among the Italian proverbs. When in doubt, raise your hat. Surely it is better to be too polite (if such a thing were possible) than to be rudely discourteous to someone.

The question of whether or not the hat should be removed in the elevator is perplexing. Some contend that the elevator is the same as a small room in a private home, and therefore that the hat should be removed. Others just as positively declare that the elevator is the same as the street, and that it is unnecessary to raise the hat. The question of drafts and colds in the head have entered into the discussion—but ultimately all writers of etiquette reach the same conclusion: as the elevator is so small and boasts a ceiling, it may be considered in the same class

196 BOOK OF ETIQUETTE

as a room, and the polite man will keep his head uncovered —especially while there are women in it. The man who is very susceptible to colds may lift his hat upon entering the car and replace it immediately. But it is not courteous to retain the hat entirely.

HOW TO RAISE THE HAT

It is not enough to know when to raise the hat, one must also know the accepted manner of doing it. Profound and elaborate bows are old-fashioned and un-American. While lifting the hat one should incline the head slightly and smile. But it must be remembered that the unmannerly habit of touching the hat, instead of lifting it is an indication of sheer laziness and a lack of gallantry.

"A hat raised half-heartedly is a courtesy without charm" is a proverb well worth remembering. Why raise your hat at all, if you do it only as an annoying duty that must be gotten over as quickly as possible? If you want to be courteous and polite show by your manner that you *are* polite. A graceful lifting of the hat is entirely incompatible with an unsmiling face. But both together—a sincere smile and a graceful lifting of the hat —are most pleasing to the person for whom the greeting is intended.

Many gentlemen, while speaking to ladies in the street, stand with their uncovered. While it is a polite custom, it is dangerous to the health and therefore should not be indulged in except in warm weather. The most usual method is to lift the hat upon meeting, slowly replace it during the conversation or while walking beside the lady, and lift it again when taking leave of her.

ON THE STREET

IN THE STREET CAR

"The world is on wheels!" declares a modern writer. "Everyone is going somewhere, and all the world is moving!" And Dr. Eliot of Harvard, in a recent newspaper article, deplores the fact that the "younger generation" is losing in courtesy and good manners that which it is gaining in this rapid onward rush of the world's affairs.

"There is a general coarsening of manners" declares the president emeritus of Harvard University. "Young women expect to encounter rudeness from young men and they do not resent it" and when one watches the rough-and-tumble manners of people in subways and street cars every day one is inclined to agree with him.

The custom of relinquishing one's seat, for instance, is not as marked as it was a decade ago. Perhaps the new suffrage amendments may have something to do with it. Perhaps the war and woman's changed status is the reason. Or it may just be a "coarsening of manners." But whatever it is, we do not find our young men of to-day as eager to relinquish their seats in the car as they were several years ago.

Women should never indicate by word or glance that they wish a man to give up his seat. But the woman who is ill, or who is extremely tired should feel no hesitancy in making the request if her need is really great. When the seat is given, the owner should be thanked for his kindness. This holds true whether the courtesy has been requested or whether it has been spontaneous.

Boisterous action in the street car is inexcusable—as it is anywhere else. The girl of mirthful disposition who laughs loudly may not be doing it to attract attention to

BOOK OF ETIQUETTE

herself but merely to give vent to her gay spirits, but it is most unattractive. "All noise is waste"—but it is more than waste in public where it reflects ill-breeding upon the person who is the perpetrator.

ENTERING THE CAR

In ascending a car on an omnibus, a man assists the woman he is escorting by a slight touch at the elbow. He enters after her, finding her a seat and taking his place next to her. If there is only one empty place in the car, he stands directly in front of her, or as near as possible. If a man relinquishes his seat to the woman, the escort must lift his hat and offer a word of thanks for the kindness. A smile from the woman is sufficient. In leaving the car the order is reversed; the gentleman leaves first and assists the woman in alighting.

A man pays all fares and fees for the woman he is escorting. But when a man meets a woman in the street by chance and they both enter a car together, he is not under obligation to pay her fare. Common sense has made a rule of its own in this matter, and some men insist upon paying the fare of women they meet even inside the car. But etiquette tells us that only an escort is under obligation to pay the fare of a woman.

IN THE TAXICAB

Here again the woman enters first, assisted by her escort. There is no rule as to which side she should take in the car; she enters first and takes the furthest seat, whether it be to the right or left. In alighting the man

ON THE STREET 199

again leads the way, assisting the woman to reach the ground safely.

A word of caution will not be amiss here. No woman or girl should ride in a taxicab with a man who is not her escort, unless she has a very good reason for doing so. It is not conventional, and in most cases it is not prudent. The woman with a fine regard for all the little niceties of good conduct, who wishes to observe the rules of etiquette in their truest sense, does not ride in a taxicab with a man, and allow him to pay the bill, unless he is acting as her escort. And ordinarily, a gentleman of polished manners does not ask a lady to ride with him unless he is taking her to a social function such as a dance, formal dinner or theater party.

If the taxicab has double seats, the man should take his place with his back facing the driver, unless he is an old friend of many years' standing. A new acquaintance should not take the liberty of sharing a seat in the taxicab with a young woman unless she has particularly asked him to do so.

SOME SOCIAL ERRORS

Reserve should not be confused with haughtiness. The first is a necessary social attribute; the second is a regrettable social evil that should be carefully avoided.

To be haughty, proud, superior, is to indicate that you hold those beneath you in contempt. When etiquette is based on courtesy and a consideration for the rights and comforts of a fellow-man, one readily sees why this is a mistake. A haughty person is a conceited person. A haughty person is an unkind person. And therefore, a haughty person is an uncultured person.

BOOK OF ETIQUETTE

Reserve, on the other hand, is a calm dignity that comes with the knowledge that one does and says only what is entirely correct. It is that certain well-poised sureness of oneself entirely devoid of all semblance of pride,—yet with sufficient self-respect to attract instinctively the respect of others. Reserve is that which is developed only after close application to, and experience in, the laws of good conduct. Haughtiness is merely a sham drapery used to cover the defects of uncultured manners.

The other extreme of haughtiness is self-consciousness. Both faults are the result of too much self-thought. To overcome self-consciousness, which makes you awkward, easily embarrassed, and ill at ease—think less of yourself! Think of the books you have read, of the people you have met, of the new scenes you have observed. Take a more keen interest in people. Speak to them. Don't be afraid of them. But most important of all, forget yourself. And before you realize it, you will have developed sufficient poise and *unself-consciousness* to be confident to appear in the most elaborate drawing-room, among the most brilliant and highly cultured people, without feeling the least bit ill at ease.

"Our personal appearance is our show window where we insert what we have for sale, and we are judged by what we put there." If you remember to observe this bit of philosophy of Orison S. Marden's—not only in dress, but in speech and manners and bearing—you will invariably do and say and wear what is correct in public.

CHAPTER V

AT THE THEATER AND THE OPERA

DRESS AT THE THEATER AND OPERA

For a matinee a simple street dress of a dark material is appropriate except during the summer months when one may wear dainty fabrics and light colors.

In the evening if one is to sit in a box one should wear evening dress, not so elaborate, however, as that worn at a ball or dance. If one is to sit in the orchestra full or semi-evening attire is appropriate but in the cheaper seats such attire is out of order. Plain street dress should be worn.

ENTERING THE THEATER

There is one law of good conduct that cannot be over-emphasized—and that is the law of making oneself inconspicuous. A man or woman who is the "center of attraction" when the occasion does not merit it, cannot claim the distinction of being entirely well-bred. There seems to be a certain dignified simplicity and modesty in dress, speech and behavior that distinguishes well-bred people and enables them to move with ease and unconscious grace among people of every status and position.

BOOK OF ETIQUETTE

ARRIVING LATE

Whether it be the theater, opera, lecture or some other public entertainment, it is exceedingly bad form to arrive late. People who are considerate always make it a point to arrive five or ten minutes before the hour set for the performance.

When one is unavoidably detained and reaches the theater after the curtain has been raised, it is polite to remain at the rear of the auditorium until the first intermission. It is permissible to take one's place quickly and quietly while the audience is applauding; but it is rude and inconsiderate to attempt to find your place while the performers are on the stage and the attention of the audience has been fixed.

It is good form for the man or woman who arrives late to excuse himself or herself to the people who are disturbed while the vacant place is being reached. One may say, "I am sorry to disturb you," or, "Pardon me." Those who are seated should rise to allow passage if the place is very narrow, but if there is sufficient room for them to pass without stumbling it is better for those who are already seated to keep their places, drawing aside to facilitate matters for the new-comers.

ABOUT WRAPS

It is customary for a woman to slip off her wrap in the lobby and carry it on her arm to her place, where it may either be placed over the back of her chair or folded in her lap. Some big theaters now have checking rooms for women, where wraps may be left until after the perform-

AT THE THEATER AND THE OPERA 203

ance. Other theaters arrange for a wrap-checking service in the ladies' dressingroom. Individual preference must decide whether the wrap shall be checked or kept with one. But to stand up after the play has begun, and leisurely divest oneself of one's wraps, is a breach of good manners. If her wrap is a light one a woman may keep it on until she is seated and then slip it off her shoulders and let it fall over the back of her chair.

Hat and veil are usually removed after one has been comfortably seated. Or, if one prefers, they may be checked in the dressingroom. In the evening, when *décolleté* is worn with an evening veil and no hat, the veil may be dropped over the shoulders and kept throughout the evening.

A very common fault is to begin to put on wraps and hats before the performance is over. This is rude to the performers and unjust to the people around you. Wraps should not be touched until the curtain has fallen for the last time, even though one is anxious to leave. Politeness is a vital law of good conduct, and certainly nothing could be more impolite than to interrupt an actor or lecturer by fussing with clothing.

Gentlemen usually check their hats and coats in the lobby; otherwise they remove them both before taking their places. The hat is deposited under the chair, and the coat may either be folded and placed over the knees, or over the back of the seat.

ORDER OF PRECEDENCE

There seems to be some doubt as to the correct order of precedence upon entering and leaving the theater or concert hall. Some authorities on etiquette claim that the

BOOK OF ETIQUETTE

correct order is for the usher to lead the way to the seats, the lady following immediately behind him, and after the lady, her escort. But more modern usage has changed this order of precedence.

To-day it is correct for the usher to lead the way, a few feet ahead of the gentleman. Immediately behind the gentleman follows the lady. The reason for this change is that it enables the gentleman to stop before their places and hand the lady to her seat. Otherwise this duty devolves upon the usher. However, as the lady precedes the gentleman in almost everything else, it is safe to assume that both methods of precedence given above are correct.

One thing is certain—it is absolutely incorrect for lady and gentleman to walk down the aisle together, arm in arm.

BEFORE THE PLAY

Upon entering a theater or concert hall a few moments before the curtain is drawn, one becomes immediately conscious of the gentle buzz of voices throughout the audience. While it is entirely permissible to carry on a conversation before the play begins, it is most offensive to those who are sitting near for one to act in a noisy, conspicuous manner. Low tones are a mark of cultivation. As a matter of fact, loud noise of any kind is an exhibition of thoughtlessness, and it can be so easily avoided by a little caution.

Another reprehensible habit often indulged in before the play is that of standing up and glancing around one in the search of a familiar face, then nodding and smiling conspicuously to a friend in some other part of the auditorium. After having once been seated one should remain so, instead of rising and disturbing others. It is

AT THE THEATER AND THE OPERA 205

merely a form of vanity to search for friends among the audience and endeavor to attract their attention.

A certain gayety of manner is, of course, in harmony with the occasion, but it should be the kind of gayety that is under control. It is commendable to be smiling and cheerful—but be careful that you do not laugh hoisterously or talk loudly.

WHEN THE CURTAIN IS DRAWN

The first chord of the orchestra should be the sign for absolute quiet in the theater. There can be nothing quite as rude as continuing a conversation while the musicians are doing their best to entertain you.

Usually, when the orchestra begins, programs are hastily opened and scanned. This causes an unpleasant rustling sound that mars the effect of the music and is sometimes very disturbing to music-lovers who are sitting near you. The time to glance through the program is while you are waiting for the play to begin, and before the musicians have taken their places. Then it should not be referred to again until during intermission.

People who arrive while the orchestra is playing should be particularly quiet. Care should be taken that chairs are not clattered or allowed to drop noisily.

DURING THE PERFORMANCE

It hardly seems necessary to say that talking or continued whispering during a performance is ill-bred and rude. Young people are most at fault in this matter. They must learn to curb their enthusiasms and criticisms until after the performance or during the intermissions.

BOOK OF ETIQUETTE

"The *intelligent* listener never interrupts" declares an eminent authority. Complete quiet should be maintained during a performance or concert; all talking or whispering is interruption. Beating time to the music, whistling or rustling programs are also unmannerly.

If anyone near you is inconsiderate enough to talk or hum during the performance, it is entirely proper to turn and in quiet tones request that he or she be more quiet. It is necessary, though that you do not speak in a curt or offensive manner that will cause antagonism on the part of the stranger. A kind request always meets with an immediate response. You might say, "Pardon me. Do you mind speaking a little lower?" or "Would you mind speaking more quietly?" It is polite, also, to offer a reason, as "I cannot hear very well. Will you please speak more softly?" If the person thus addressed complies with your request and answers you politely, you should acknowledge it with a very courteous "Thank you." But there should be no further conversation during the performance.

THE OFFENDING HAT

The polite woman removes her hat as soon as she is comfortably seated. To wear a hat that obstructs the view of the people behind is inconsiderate—and anything that is inconsiderate is also ill-bred.

If you find that it is necessary to ask the woman sitting before you to remove her hat, be sure that you couch your request in terms of careful politeness. This is very important. The cultured man or woman is polite at all times, and especially so when reminding someone of a politeness that has been overlooked. It should be remem-

AT THE THEATER AND THE OPERA 207

bered that a hearty smile and a friendly manner go a long way in winning a similar response.

"Pardon me, madam, but may I ask that you remove your hat?" is the form usually used. But a better way is to offer some explanation, as, "I am sorry to disturb you, but your hat is in my way. Will you kindly remove it?" The simple form "Will you please remove your hat?" is sufficient if it is accompanied by a pleasant smile. But under no circumstances is a curt, "Take off your hat" permissible. If one hesitates to speak to a stranger he or she may call the usher and request him to ask the offender to remove her hat.

The woman thus addressed may, upon complying with the request, either smile and remain silent, or say simply, "Yes, indeed." Other forms frequently used are "Certainly," "I am sorry," or, "Pardon me" The two latter forms are perhaps the best, for they indicate that the offender realizes her lack of politeness and is sorry.

APPLAUSE

Clapping hands is a natural language of delight. Very young infants clap their hands when they are happy. Children clap their hands to express their pleasure. And older people clap their hands to show appreciation and enjoyment.

But stamping of feet, whistling, or noisy acclamation of any kind is bad form. This may seem superfluous in a book of etiquette, but it is surprising how many otherwise cultured men stamp noisily or whistle when something said or done upon the stage particularly pleases them.

Ill-timed or continual applause is disturbing to performers and audience alike. Indiscriminate hand-clapping

208 BOOK OF ETIQUETTE

is not only annoying, but reflects poor judgment upon the offender. When you feel that an actor or lecturer merits applause, give him a short and hearty hand-clapping, but do not make the mistake of clapping noisily and excessively each time the opportunity presents itself.

It should be particularly remembered that ill-timed applause hinders the progress of the performers. '

DURING INTERMISSION

At a theater party, when there are several men and women in the party, the men may take advantage of the intermission to leave their places for a few moments. But they must not indulge in this privilege more than once during a performance, if they wish to be polite and considerate to the ladies. And they should not go without excusing themselves to the ladies whom they are escorting.

When a young man and woman are together, it is the height of ill-breeding for him to leave her alone during intermission. If he wishes water or candy or programs, the usher will attend to it for him. He must not leave the lady alone unless she requests him to get something for her. A gentleman alone may, of course, come and go as he pleases during intermission.

If one must walk past strangers to leave one's seat for intermission, or if one wishes to leave before the performance is over, a courteous apology must be made to the people who are disturbed. "I beg your pardon," or, "May I trouble you to pass?" are the forms most frequently used. When the aisle is reached, it is polite to acknowledge the obligation by smiling and saying, "Thank you."

During intermission it is permissible to step across the

Photo by George H. Davis, Jr.

Courtesy of the *Woman's Home Companion*.

AT THE THEATER AND THE OPERA 209

aisle or into another box to greet a friend. Often introductions are made, but they are not formal and need not gain future recognition. As soon as the curtain begins to rise, the caller must return to his own place.

LEAVING THE THEATER

If you wish your acquaintances to recognize your charm and cultivation, you should conduct yourself at the conclusion of the performance with the same quiet dignity that you observed when you entered the theater and while you were waiting for it to begin. Speak in low tones, smile but do not laugh, discuss the play but do it in so quiet a manner that no one but your companion will hear you. It is bad form to gather in small groups and discuss the play in loud tones. Leave the theater as quickly as possible. The attendants are waiting to close it.

It usually takes a long time for a large theater to be emptied because many inconsiderate people block the aisles and loiter at the rear of the auditorium. As soon as the curtain has fallen for the last time, gather your wraps together, slip them on if it is convenient and move quickly down the aisle to the rear. Then pass quickly out of the theater and out of the way. But if you still carry your wraps, you may either go to the dressing-room or remain a moment or two in the lobby until you have arranged them.

Shakespeare said, "All the world's a stage." If this is true, do we not owe the stage the same courtesy, respect and honor that we owe the world of fellow-men? Be as well-mannered and courteous at the theater and opera as you would in the most fastidious drawing-room.

CHAPTER VI

HOTEL ETIQUETTE

AT THE HOTEL

There is a very distinct code of ethics by which the lady and gentleman must be governed when stopping at a hotel. It is a mistaken idea that one may act as one pleases, merely because the hotel is public. But it is as important to remember one's social obligations as it is in the home of a friend.

Indeed, the hotel is one place where men and women are most likely to make embarrassing blunders and commit humiliating mistakes. This is especially true of the man or woman from a small town who stops for a day or two at a big hotel in the city. Only by knowing thoroughly the laws of good conduct, as adapted to hotel life, can one expect to move smoothly and with ease through its often puzzling social intricacies.

At home, or even when visiting at a friend's home, a boor may remain undetected. But how quickly the truth appears after he has registered at a hotel! There are numerous little tests of good breeding that betray him; the servants themselves soon discover whether or not he is cultivated, well-bred. And they invariably treat him accordingly.

The definite rules will be given in the following paragraphs. But for one's general conduct it should be re-

HOTEL ETIQUETTE 211

membered solely that the hospitality of a hotel is no less worthy of courtesy and consideration than the hospitality extended by a friend.

THE WOMAN GUEST

To-day women stop at hotels much more frequently than they did a decade ago. The war brought with it a widened horizon for the women of America, and they travel all over the country on political, professional and business enterprises as well as for pleasure. It is, cousequently, necessary for them to stop often at hotels; thus they must know exactly how to conduct themselves.

Some hotels, in smaller towns, have ladies' entrances The woman visitor should first ascertain whether or not there are such entrances, and if so should govern her actions accordingly. But in large cities, hotels generally have but one large entrance where the woman may enter without embarrassment. Business often takes the modern woman into strange towns, and there is no reason why she should feel the least hesitancy in stopping at a hotel—providing she knows how to conduct herself.

Hand baggage should be relinquished at the door to attendants of the hotel. The woman should make her way immediately to the desk-clerk, register, and then follow the page assigned to her, to her room. It is not good form to loiter in the lobby before going to one's room after one has registered. A wise plan is to call the hotel on the telephone beforehand, requesting them to reserve a room or suite of rooms as the case may be. This will eliminate any possibility of having to leave the hotel because there is no room. It is always a wise plan for a woman to reserve a room in advance, especially if she is

212 BOOK OF ETIQUETTE

to arrive late at night since certain hostelries refuse to admit women after a certain hour.

The day of the chaperon is practically over, except in the cases of very young girls. But women to-day travel very often in the company of their maids. Whether one double room or two single rooms adjoining each other are chosen, depends upon the degree of intimacy between mistress and maid, and also upon convenience and accommodation at the hotel. The usual form is to reserve two adjoining rooms.

A woman never stops at a hotel without baggage. Even though she intends to stay only over-night, she should carry a small handbag with her. A woman traveling across country with a great deal of baggage may have her trunks sent on ahead to the hotel if she reserves rooms previously. On no occasion should the woman approach the clerk's desk laden with valises and bags. A hotel attendant should take them from the car and deposit them on the floor near the desk; or the guest's chauffeur should deposit them at the entrance of the hotel, to be attended to by one of the hotel attendants.

RECEIVING MASCULINE GUESTS

A gentleman calling upon a lady who is stopping at a hotel, gives his name to the desk clerk. It is not necessary to offer a card. The form in most common usage is, "Mr. Roberts to see Miss Nelson." The clerk will call Miss Nelson on the telephone or will direct him to one of the telephones in the lobby, and advise her of the visitor. If she is ill and does not wish to see him, she will say, "Please tell Mr. Roberts I am indisposed and I am sorry that I cannot see him to-day." But she should

HOTEL ETIQUETTE 213

not refuse to see a visitor without offering some sort of legitimate excuse. If she is not ready to greet visitors, she may say to the clerk, "Tell Mr. Roberts I shall be downstairs in a half-hour." That is the maximum amount of time it is permissible to keep a visitor waiting.

Ladies receive the gentlemen who call on them in the parlor or reception room of the hotel. They may be hatless and gloveless, if they wish, observing the same rules of etiquette that they would observe in their drawing-room at home. But if the visits are entirely of a business nature, it is always advisable for the woman to wear a hat.

To welcome a man in one's room is to break a convention that has many years of strict practice to uphold it. It is a serious blunder in hotel etiquette.

If a gentleman calls upon a lady at a hotel, whether it be in a business or social capacity, and finds that she is not in, he may leave his card with the desk clerk to be forwarded to her. It is necessary, however, that he write on the back of the card for whom it is intended; for the memories of desk clerks are not quite as retentive as some of us think they are, and there is a possibility of the card being sent to the wrong guest.

MAKING FRIENDS AT THE HOTEL

Hotels have the alarming propensity of making one feel extremely lonely, especially if one is stopping there all by oneself. And there is the very strong temptation to forget all about conventionalities and speak to the friendly-looking old gentleman at the next table, or the charming young woman in the dressing-room. But every-

214 BOOK OF ETIQUETTE

one, and the woman especially, should be extremely careful in making friends and acquaintances at the hotel.

Self-introductions are not unusual at the hotel. In the
dining-room, in the lobby, in the rest-rooms, conversations
are often started that result in self-introductions and
subsequent acquaintanceships. But one should be prudent. It is not wise to go beyond the usual civilities of
greetings and casual conversations or to take anyone
into your confidence.

While conducting yourself with all due courtesy and
consideration for the hospitality extended by the hotel,
it is important to remember that after all the hotel is not
a private home, but a temporary one for travelers—for
the public. The conventions you observe in public must
therefore also be observed at the hotel. Strangers still
remain strangers, even though you sleep under the same
roof with them.

If a gentleman becomes interested in another gentleman, either in the hotel lobby or the dining-room, and he
wishes to become acquainted with him either for business
or social reasons, he may request the manager of the
hotel to make the necessary introduction. He may also
indulge in the self-introduction, but it is never as effective as the introduction made by a third person.

HOW TO REGISTER

It is not considered dignified for a woman traveling
alone to sign herself in the hotel register without the title
of "Mrs." or "Miss." A married woman should register as
"Mrs. Harris K. Jennings," an unmarried woman as
"Miss Mildred Jennings." It is decidedly bad form to

HOTEL ETIQUETTE 215

sign oneself "Millie Jennings," or "Flossie Jennings" for Florence. The full first and last name should be written out and preceded by the correct title of "Miss" or "Mrs." Only the eldest daughter, or only daughter, of a family may sign herself, "Miss Jennings."

When traveling together, a mother and daughter register as "Mrs. Harris K. Jennings, Miss Mildred Jennings." Even a very young girl is registered in this manner. A small boy's name appears in the register as "Master Edward Jennings." A husband and wife register as "Mr. and Mrs. Harris K. Jennings." To use the expression "Mr. Harris K. Jennings and wife" is considered very bad form indeed. Only those who are ignorant of the best rules of hotel etiquette make this blunder.

After the name, the town and state from which the visitors have come should be written in the register. Thus the complete entry of a young lady would be, "Miss Mildred Jennings, Cambridge, Mass." A gentleman would register in this manner, "Mr. Harris K. Jennings, 681 Fifth Ave., New York." Even if he lives in New York and stops at a hotel in that city, he must write "New York" after his name. Nor is it correct for him to omit the "Mr." from before his name.

Deep flourishes and illegible handwriting should be avoided. The well-bred man or woman registers neatly in a clear, small, legible script.

IN THE PUBLIC DINING-ROOM

"A gentleman is known by the way he eats," declared a well-known writer recently in one of his newspaper articles. And this is particularly true in the hotel dining-

216 BOOK OF ETIQUETTE

room, where one is judged—or misjudged—by one's table manners; and one should remember to make them as gracefully correct as if the dinner were a most formal one in a private home.

If you drop a fork or other part of the table service, do not stoop to pick it up. Simply ignore the incident and leave it to the waiter to attend to. A most reprehensible habit is to pick up a knife or fork that has been dropped, wipe it carefully with the napkin, and proceed to use it. The correct thing to do is to leave the fork or knife on the floor where it has fallen and request another one from the waiter in charge.

It is optional with the ladies whether or not they wear their hats to dinner. In the dining-rooms of the larger hotels, however, women generally do not appear hatless. Even though one is a permanent guest and a special table is reserved for one each evening, it is better to wear a hat to dinner at the hotel.

Loud laughing and talking reflect ill-manners. And this applies not only to the dining-room, but to the private rooms as well. As a rule, the partitions in hotels are thin and talking that is the least bit loud can be heard in the next room. For this reason, it is also discourteous to play any musical instrument at such times of the day when it would be likely to disturb those whose rooms adjoin. At the table, conversation may be conducted only when low, natural tones of voice are used. Loud talking should be avoided.

Guests who wish to eat in their rooms should request that a waiter be sent to the room with a menu. The order is given, and the waiter will see that it is satisfactorily filled. For this service he should receive an extra fee from the guest.

HOTEL ETIQUETTE

HOTEL STATIONERY

Hotels invariably place a supply of writing paper in the room. This is meant for the business or social correspondence of the guest. More of this paper is usually found in the writing-room.

Do not waste the hotel stationery. Use it only if you have to. You would not waste the stationery provided for your use at the home of your friend. Then why take advantage of the courtesies extended by your hotel? Just as one adapts oneself to the routine at the home of a friend, so should one accustom and adapt oneself to the rules and regulations of the hotel.

Never take any of the hotel stationery away with you. It is as wrong in principle as carrying away one of the Turkish towels. Use only as much as you need for your correspondence, and leave the rest behind you.

REGARDING THE SERVANTS

Arrogance is only another form of selfish pride. The man or woman who is cultured is never arrogant. After all, isn't it sham—sham adopted to cover the defects of manner and bearing?

If you are dissatisfied with some service performed by one of the hotel attendants, if one of them is inattentive to your wants or negligible in his duties, complain to the manager. Do not scold the servants themselves, or order them in a peremptory manner to do such and such a thing correctly. The greatest vulgarity—and you will do well to remember this—is to look down upon a person as inferior merely because he or she has to earn his or her

218   **BOOK OF ETIQUETTE**

own living.   There is nothing to be ashamed of in good, honest, faithful toil.   But the person who ridicules it has a great deal to be ashamed of.

Be considerate to the hotel attendants.   Do not expect the maid to come hurrying to your room when you ring at one o'clock in the morning.   The guest who is kind and thoughtful will receive twice as much service as the person who is constantly complaining and scolding.

LEAVING THE HOTEL

When you are ready to leave the hotel, call an attendant to carry your baggage down to the entrance.   Do not attempt to carry it down yourself, whether you are a man or woman, unless you have only one or two small valises.

Different hotels have different rules with regard to keys. Some require that the key be returned to the desk clerk. Others require that it be left in the room.   When in doubt, the best form is to return the key at the desk before asking the cashier for one's bill.   After this is paid, ring for a servant to call a car; never do this yourself.

Tipping, though an entirely un-American custom, is still widely practiced.   When leaving the hotel, it is necessary to tip, or fee, those hotel attendants who have been of service.

CHAPTER VII

TRAVEL ETIQUETTE

THE RESTLESS URGE OF TRAVEL

Man is essentially a restless being. Ever since the world began, men and women have found themselves growing impatient, eager for new scenes, new faces, new experiences. First they packed up their few belongings and moved by foot to another place a few miles away. Then they took down their tents and put them up in some other place. Soon we find them building houses, and at different periods moving to other houses. Grad ally, through the ages, as man's desire for wider experiences and a wider radius for travel and exploration developed, the horse-drawn carriage appeared, then the steamboat, then the locomotive, the surface car, the subway, the auto-mobile and airplane.

Diogenes with his lantern could not find an honest man, and he would have just as difficult a task to-day to find a man, woman or child who does not love to travel. Everyone likes to see new scenes, meet new people, enjoy new experiences; and the easiest way to accomplish this is through traveling.

THE CUSTOMS OF COUNTRIES

In America, where almost everyone is something of a tourist, the etiquette of travel must not be neglected. And

BOOK OF ETIQUETTE

it is particularly important that the customs of foreign countries be respected, especially now that the world is becoming one great family and intercourse among the nations is increasing every day.

Somehow, we Americans feel that there is no other country in the world quite as wonderful as our dear United States. There is, of course, no reason why we should not believe this; but it is bad form and poor judgment to show by action and speech in other countries that you believe it. The man or woman who affects a supercilious disdain of all foreign countries and their forms and customs, is not impressing the natives with his vast superiority, but is really convincing them that he or she is an ill-bred simpleton. And even our beloved America is hardly perfect enough to warrant a great deal of boasting.

In traveling abroad, every national prejudice, every custom of every little town or village, should be observed as nearly as possible. "When in Rome do as the Romans do" is the truest courtesy that can be observed by those who travel. Well-bred and polite people conform to native customs no matter how strange they may appear. And they do it gracefully, with a smile of friendliness rather than one of disdain.

In her book "Fear and Conventionality," Elsie Parsons relates an incident during her visit to Tokyo. She and her companions were the guests of Japan. As they were on their way to the station, the natives stole up furtively and placed cards in their carriages. Realizing that it must be some native custom, the occupants of the carriages merely smiled and allowed the cards to remain. Perhaps if they had been haughty individuals they might have scowled at the seeming intrusion, thrown aside the cards, and won the everlasting hate of the natives not

TRAVEL ETIQUETTE 221

only for themselves but for all future American tourists.
For one ill-bred traveler makes it hard for the next people who pass along the same route, however courteous
they may be. The best way to make a pleasant journey is
to adapt oneself graciously and courteously to varying
circumstances and conditions.

THE TRAVELER'S WARDROBE

It is not wise to overburden oneself with numerous
clothes when traveling. Wardrobes can always be re-
plenished if the necessity arises, in other countries, and
there is really no need to impede one's journey with numerous trunks and handbags that must be constantly
checked, looked after and traced. Many people have
journeyed happily all over Europe with only a suit case
or two.

Women should dress quietly and inconspicuously when
traveling. A dark, tailored suit with light blouses is in
excellent taste, especially when worn with a small dark
turban or toque. In her wardrobe should be simple, but
smart frocks for the afternoon, an evening gown, numerous fresh blouses and perhaps a sport outfit or two. An
abundant supply of fresh undergarments is essential, but
even these can be bought during the trip if the supply
does not hold out. Remember that it is a wise rule to
take too little rather than too much. An experienced
traveler can usually be distinguished by the small amount
of luggage he carries.

The wardrobe of the gentleman traveling should also
be as small as possible. Of course the number of suits
and the quantity of linen he takes with him depends upon
the length of his trip and the social activities he expects
to indulge in.

222 BOOK OF ETIQUETTE

If the trip is to be one of long duration the porter will provide a paper bag in which the hat may be placed. On a trip of this kind it is permissible to make oneself at ease by removing hat and wraps and leaning against a pillow which the porter will furnish upon request.

IN THE TRAIN

An ill-bred person is always known by his selfishness and discourtesy in the train. He will claim more service and comfort than he is entitled to. He will scold the attendants and make himself generally a nuisance. He will encroach upon the rights of others, assume an air of importance, and make himself conspicuous by his actions and manners.

When in the train, be as solicitous of the passenger's comforts as you would be of your dearest friend's, if he or she were traveling with you. Do not keep your window open if you know that it is causing discomfort to others. Do not spread your hand-luggage into the aisles where other passengers will be likely to trip over it. It is good nature, courtesy and an affable adaptation to unexpected circumstances that mark the lady and gentleman in traveling.

If someone opens a window that places you in a draught or exposes you to flying cinders or other discomforts, it is permissible to request politely that the window be lowered again. The courteous man or woman will do so immediately without impatience or annoyance.

All boisterous behavior, loud laughing and talking, are as reprehensible in the train as they are in the drawing-room. Composure of manner and a calm, easy grace distinguish the cultured traveler. He who is restless, excit-

TRAVEL ETIQUETTE 223

able, fidgety, who talks in loud tones, walks back and forth to the water cooler many times, arranges and rearranges his belongings, is merely advertising to the other passengers in the train that he is traveling for the first time, and that he does not know how to conduct himself.

It should be remembered that the railroad train is a public place, and therefore it is not correct to discuss family affairs or converse loudly about people who are absent while you are traveling on it. This habit of talking about people who are absent is most uncivil. How often do we overhear conversations in which some unfortunate man or woman is "picked to pieces" by inconsiderate friends or acquaintances who mean no harm and bear no malice but having nothing else to talk about, choose their friend as the subject of their conversation. It is unkind, and it is certainly bad form.

IN THE SLEEPING CAR

In traveling on the sleeping car the person who has the lower berth is entitled to the seat facing forward while the one with the upper berth has the seat facing backward. If a lady was unable to procure a lower berth and the gentleman beneath her offers to exchange she may at discretion accept the offer.

When one is ready to go to bed he rings for the porter to prepare the berth. In crowded trains it may be some time before this can be done and the owner of the berth must be patient until his turn comes. It is courteous to consult one's seat mate before asking to have the beds made for the night, and if one wishes to go to bed early because of fatigue or slight illness, he may politely beg of his partner to allow him to do so.

224 BOOK OF ETIQUETTE

The person who is to spend the night on the train should provide himself with a dressing gown, a traveling toilette case containing the necessary accessories such as brushes, soap, tooth-paste, pins, etc. One may dress and undress in the regular dressing room but many people prefer to accomplish the greater part of their toilette in their berths. It is not permissible to take exclusive possession of the dressing-room or to spread one's belongings out so as to be in the way of the other travelers.

TRAIN COURTESY

A gentleman always steps aside to permit a woman to enter a train first. He does not rush ahead of her for a choice seat, nor does he open a window near her without having first requested and obtained her permission to do so.

Civility of the highest sort is possible when traveling in a train. One may be courteous to the gruff ticket-collector and polite to the bustling expressman. A "soft answer turneth away wrath"—and we usually find that a curt, peremptory order receives response that is no less curt; but a kind and courteous request invariably receives an immediate friendly response. "Thank you" is never superfluous, and it is only the exceedingly impolite man who fails to say it when some service, no matter how trivial, has been performed for him.

When a gentleman sees that a woman passenger is having difficulty in raising a window, he need feel no hesitancy in offering to assist her. However, the courtesy ends when the window has been raised; he resumes his seat and the incident is closed. It is incorrect for him to

TRAVEL ETIQUETTE 225

attempt a conversation with her or to intrude upon her in any way. The gentleman should also offer his seat to a woman standing in an overcrowded train, or to a man very much older than himself. A man or woman carrying a child should never be permitted to remain standing.

A gentleman never allows a woman to feel incumbent upon him for monetary assistance. For instance, if a young and inexperienced woman is traveling alone and seems to be in doubt as to where she will be able to get something to eat, the gentleman may offer to send a porter to take her order. Or if no porter can be found, he may himself get her a sandwich and a glass of milk. But he must absolutely accept the money expended for these articles, otherwise the young woman will undoubtedly feel embarrassed.

THE WOMAN TRAVELER

Women travel about much more independently to-day than ever before. We find young and elderly women traveling across country for business purposes, for relaxation, and for pleasure. And though conventions are no less strict than they were twenty-five years ago, these women who travel are enjoying a much wider and more untrammeled freedom than their grandmothers ever enjoyed.

Women who have not had much experience in traveling, who are ignorant of the laws of good conduct while *en route,* are prone to expect a great many courtesies and much attention from the train officials and from the gentlemen passengers. Very often they make themselves appear rude and ill-bred by their assumed manner of haughtiness. It is the quiet, dignified manner that com-

226 BOOK OF ETIQUETTE

mands respect; not the exacting, fault-finding and im-
perious one that so many women like to affect.

The woman on a train should never sacrifice the comfort of the people around her for her own. It is exceedingly discourteous to insist upon having a window
open, when you know that others around you object, even
though they are all men. And it is just as discourteous
to accept a seat that a gentleman has kindly relinquished,
or to accept any other courtesy, without offering polite
thanks.

It is bad form to get excited over every little thing
that happens. A two-minute delay, a brief unexplained
stop, is enough to make some women fret and fume.

The woman who travels alone should maintain a great
deal of dignity and reserve. She should not make an
acquaintance of any fellow-passengers of either sex, and
she should not accept courtesies from anyone without cordial thanks. But beyond those few conventional words of
thanks, there should be no conversation with a man or
woman she does not know. And yet, when the journey is
a very long one, lasting perhaps more than a day, what
harm can it be for a woman to chat a bit about the scenery or the newest "best-seller" with the motherly looking
woman beside her? Common-sense is often the better
part of etiquette.

THE WOMAN WHO TRAVELS WITH AN ESCORT

When a man serves as escort to a woman who is traveling by train, he incurs all expenses. He buys her ticket
at the station, attends to the checking and directing of
her luggage, carries her hand-bags and sees that she is
comfortably seated. He pays for all magazines and news-

TRAVEL ETIQUETTE 227

papers that she wishes and fees the porter that has helped her. He also buys and pays for all refreshments taken during the trip.

A lady invariably precedes her escort down the aisle of the train. She takes the inside seat and leaves the arranging of the luggage and wraps to the gentleman. He may, if he excuses himself, spend part of the trip in the smoking car, but it is exceedingly rude of him to leave the lady by herself throughout the trip. In fact, it is wise after the first few hours of travel, to leave the lady to her own devices for she may want to nap or to read a book. Even one's dearest friend, or one's favorite brother can become monotonous and tiresome after four or five hours of continuous conversation on a noisy train.

IN THE DINING-CAR

When a man meets a woman on a train, and after a brief conversation, invites her into the dining-car, she may assume that he wishes to be the host and that he would be offended if she refused to allow him to pay for her meal. However, the woman who travels alone must be extremely circumspect in her conduct, and she must not incur monetary obligations from men who are almost strangers to her.

For instance, if a man and woman who have met just once before and who are not really friends but slight acquaintances, find that they are traveling to the same place at the same time, they may for mutual pleasure's sake, elect to travel together. This is especially true when the journey is one of four or five hours' duration, when a bit of conversation would enliven the monotony of the trip. In this case, if both decide to go into the dining-room together, the woman must by no means allow the

BOOK OF ETIQUETTE

man to pay her bill. He may pay the tip, if he wishes, but he must accept the money that she offers him to pay for her share of the bill. A considerate woman will wait until they are back at their seats before venturing to reimburse her companion. It is better to have the waiter present separate bills. This does away with all awkwardness and embarrassment.

A gentleman who is escorting a lady on a trip should not be expected to pay for her meals on the train, unless there is only one and he feels that it would be a pleasure for him to serve as host on that occasion. But if the trip lasts several days, the woman should insist that she pay her own expenses. This is especially important if the escort is a friend and not a relative; she should by no means allow him to pay her bills.

CHILDREN ON THE TRAIN

Very often it is necessary for parents to travel with their children. The mother must see that her youngsters observe the most careful order while they are in the train and that they do not disturb the other passengers.

It is not very pleasant for young children to sit quietly for three or four hours, and the wise mother will see that they have something to amuse themselves with. A big picture book for the boy, a doll for the girl or some other equally interesting diversion will keep the child from becoming impatient and restless.

It is very wrong to permit children to race up and down the aisles, to climb over the backs of the seats, to play noisy games or in any other manner disturb the other passengers. Nor is it proper for them to eat continually, crumbling cake and dropping fruit stones upon the floor of the train. Correct, well-bred little boys and girls will

TRAVEL ETIQUETTE - 229

remain quietly seated in their places, watching the scenery or looking at the pictures in the book; and if they converse at all, it will be in a low tone that does not annoy the man or woman in front who is reading. It is never too early to teach children the golden rule of courtesy and respect.

If a child is addressed by a kindly neighbor, he should answer politely; but he must not leave his place and go over to that neighbor to be flattered and indulged, and perhaps plied with sweets that will do him more harm than good. Courtesies extended children should be gratefully acknowledged both by the child himself and by his mother.

IN THE TAXI CAB

When one arrives at a station one usually has to summon a taxi to the hotel. It is hardly safe for a young woman traveling alone at night to ride in a taxi by herself especially if the ride is to be a long one. The best way to avoid it is for her if possible to time her trip so as to arrive in the day time. If this cannot be done she must perforce accept the alternative.

If a man and woman are traveling together he helps her in before getting in himself. At the end of the ride he first helps her out and then pays and tips the driver. Ten per cent. of the amount of the fare is the usual rate. Unless a man is acting as a woman's escort he should not pay her fare.

BON VOYAGE GIFTS

Many people like to send their friends *bon voyage* gifts of flowers, books, fruit or candy when they are going away. Steamer letters are always acceptable and if they

BOOK OF ETIQUETTE

are arranged in some novel way they may be most delightful. A series of letters or small packages, one to be opened each day, go a long way toward relieving the tedium of the journey. Similar gifts may be sent to friends who are going on a long railway trip. The address of packages sent to steamers should include the name of the vessel and of the line to which it belongs and the number of the pier.

ON BOARD THE SHIP

The only place where formal introductions are not necessary is at sea. Life on shipboard is more or less free from conventionality, fortunately, especially for those who are making the voyage alone. The days would be long and tedious if one refused to speak to any of the other passengers because they had not been formally presented. It is quite permissible, if one feels so inclined, to speak to the person whose steamer chair is near or to the people who share one's table in the ship's dining-room.

COURTESY ON THE SHIP

Although the barriers of social etiquette are let down on board the ship to the extent of permitting passengers to talk to one another without formal introductions, there is no excuse for lack of courtesy. The man or woman who encroaches upon the rights of other passengers, who is discourteous or rude, will undoubtedly be shunned and avoided by the others.

It is, for instance, very bad form to use someone else's pillow, deck-chair or book, without having first requested permission to do so. It is also impolite to speak in loud

TRAVEL ETIQUETTE   231

tones, or to read aloud, where it would disturb others who are trying to nap or to read. Noisy conduct of any kind is an evidence of ill-breeding, and it is only the extremely ill-bred people who will sit in little groups and discuss and comment upon each passenger on board the ship.

Passengers are never permitted to interfere with the mechanisms of the ship. Not only is it very incorrect to do so, but it may be criminal or unsafe. To inspect certain parts of the ship barred to all but employees is to risk one's own life and the lives of the other passengers. Remain in your stateroom or on deck, but do not wander into places where ship-ethics forbid you.

THE WOMAN CROSSING THE OCEAN

It is not usual for a woman to travel across the ocean alone. But very often a young woman correspondent or journalist, or perhaps a woman buyer for some large fashion establishment, finds that business takes her abroad. She need feel no hesitancy or embarrassment in attempting the trip, if she knows and understands all the little rules of good conduct that govern railroad, steamship and hotel etiquette.

The young lady who is alone, should be careful that she does not make haphazard acquaintances among the gentlemen on board the ship. It is much wiser for her to find companions among the women passengers, and later they will undoubtedly introduce her to their gentleman acquaintances. She must never allow a man whose acquaintance she made only on board the ship, to assume any of her expenses. Nor should she sit up on the deck after eleven o'clock with one of her new acquaintances.

BOOK OF ETIQUETTE

She must be extremely careful of her conduct, and she must not give anyone the opportunity to talk about her and comment upon the fact that she is traveling without a chaperon.

When there is a dance on board the ship, the woman who is traveling alone may accept an invitation to dance from a gentleman she has not formally met; but it is always wiser to find some excuse to avoid dancing with a man who is a total stranger.

A CONCERT AT SEA

Very often, as the sea voyage draws near an end, a concert or entertainment is held for the benefit of some special charity fund, or merely for the amusement of the passengers. All those who are accomplished in any way —who can sing, dance, recite or play a musical instrument, are expected to volunteer their services for the occasion. Those who are specially requested to do so, should consent amiably; it is very rude, indeed, to refuse without some very good reason.

The passenger who absents himself from the concert which all other passengers attend, is both impolite and ill-bred. Whether he cares to or not, he should attend for the sake of courtesy. And everyone should contribute to the fund if one is raised after the concert. Only a very selfish and unkind person will refuse to contribute to a fund of this kind.

AT THE JOURNEY'S END

In the excitement of reaching *terra firma* once again, a few people are inclined to forget the courtesies due the other passengers.

TRAVEL ETIQUETTE

A little while before the ship reaches the dock, cordial farewells should be made to all those with whom one has been friendly. Hand-shaking is in order, and a polite phrase, such as, "Good-by, Mrs. Jones, I hope I shall have the pleasure of seeing you again," is most appropriate. If it is desired, an exchange of cards may accompany this leave-taking, especially if one really wishes to continue the friendship.

Farewells on board a ship should be brief but cordial. Long, sentimental farewells should never be indulged in for, at the most, they cause only sorrow at the parting of a brief friendship that may perhaps never be resumed. A warm handclasp, a sincere word or two of farewell— and it should be over.

AT HOTEL AND RESTAURANT

When arriving in a strange city, a traveler immediately asks to be driven to whatever hotel he has previously decided upon. Here he registers, using the same form that appears on his visiting card but adding to it the name of the city from which he has come.

The woman who is traveling alone does well to wire or phone ahead to the hotel and request that they reserve a room for her. While at the hotel, her conduct must be unimpeachable. She must not entertain masculine visitors in her private rooms, but only in the public reception room of the hotel. She must not return to the hotel after midnight, and she should not dine alone in the hotel dining-room after eight o'clock.

When a large party is to dine at a hotel, the table should be reserved and the dishes chosen in advance. This will save a great deal of confusion and waste of time.

234   BOOK OF ETIQUETTE

If the dinner is not arranged for in advance, the host or hostess should do all the ordering, subjecting it, of course, to the approval of the guests.

AT TEA-ROOM AND ROOF GARDEN

There seems to be something about a **tea-room**, whether it be at home or in some strange city or town, that is conducive to quiet and peacefulness. Loud talking and boisterous laughter is entirely out of place, and those who are guilty of indulging in these two improprieties condemn themselves as ill-bred.

At the tea-room the lady always retains her hat. Gloves are removed and wraps may either be slipped off the shoulders or completely removed. At the roof garden, hats are also worn, except in the evening when full evening dress is worn. Here also, it is important that a quiet reserve of manner characterize the lady and the gentleman. No amount of frivolity and gayety in the atmosphere of one's environment can excuse noisy, ill-mannered conduct.

TO THOSE WHO LOVE TO TRAVEL

Almost everyone enjoys traveling, but there are comparatively few people who really appreciate it. To those who love to travel, who find it an inspiration and a delight, the following bits of information may be of interest.

If you want to enjoy a trip to a foreign country—let us say France,—spend a week or two reading about the history and literature of that country. Make notes while you are reading, give your imagination full rein, and ab-

TRAVEL ETIQUETTE 235

sorb just as much knowledge as you can of the habits and customs of the French people. The cultivation of the imagination is especially important; while you read about France, picture the tiny villages and big cities to yourself, try to visualize the people and their homes. And when you do arrive in France, you will find keen enjoyment in seeing the people and places that lived first in your imagination. We promise that you will enjoy your trip a great deal more than if you neglected to devote a little time to the reading up of the important facts about the country you intended to visit.

Another very good plan is to buy a French-and-English or a Spanish-and-English dictionary before or as soon as reaching those countries. Whether one knows the language or not, it is always safest to have one of these little volumes handy. They are absolutely indispensable to those who expect to travel in a country the language of which is entirely unknown to them.

Wise tourists carry a map of the countries they intend visiting. It saves them much time, and often prevents mistakes. These maps may be obtained of most reliable stationers, and they take up very little space. There are times, during the journey, when their help is well nigh invaluable; and a map is nearly always a safer guide than a native.

A camera is a splendid thing to have along on one's trips abroad. No matter how vivid an impression a certain scene makes upon one's mind, it is bound to fade with the passing of a year or so. But a clear snap-shot taken of that scene will keep it fresh indefinitely, for one needs only to glance at the picture to have all associations with the scene recalled. The latest cameras have a device for writing the date and name of the place on the

BOOK OF ETIQUETTE

negative, to be printed with the picture. It is most convenient for the tourist.

There are too many of us who rush through the world seeing nothing. We race through one country after another, hustling and bustling, feeling important and acting the part—and we feel that we have traveled. But that is not travel. True travel is when a man or woman visits a strange country and carries back with him, or her, to be remembered forever, impressions of the people and customs of that country—valuable impressions that make his or her life fuller, wider, more in sympathy with the great world of fellow-men. Better stay at home and read good books about foreign countries, than rush through them with unseeing eyes, merely to be able to tell those at home that you have "been abroad."

CHAPTER VIII

TIPPING

AN UN-AMERICAN CUSTOM

Everyone knows that tipping is a European custom and is entirely un-American in principle. But while the custom is observed as widely in this country as it is to-day, it is both inconsiderate and bad form to ignore it. The wages of waiters and waitresses, porters and hotel servants are outrageously small, for the reason that they receive tips for each service they perform for individual guests and travelers. If the tipping custom were abolished, the wages of these people would be correspondingly increased; but as things are now, it is inconsiderate to deprive them of the tips that both they and their employers expect that they will receive.

In a little tea shop in Fifth Avenue in New York, the following is printed on the back of each menu "Tipping is an un-American custom. Help us abolish it by adding 10c to the amount of your bill. At the end of the week, the waiter will receive the entire amount added to his wages." Patrons have greeted this plan enthusiastically. They feel that it presages the ultimate abolition of a custom that has long been in disrepute because it is so distinctly un-American. The waiters in this progressive little tea-room serve each patron with the same degree of

BOOK OF ETIQUETTE

courtesy and respect; there is no fawning servility, no unfair dividing of service between two patrons.

Let us hope that before long all restaurants and hotels will follow the lead of the little tea-shop that revolts against the undemocratic custom of tipping. But for the present, while it remains a national custom, we must know when to tip and how to tip, and the correct amounts.

In certain states, as in South Carolina, tipping is illegal. In this case as in all others of a like nature, the rules of etiquette are set aside in favor of the statutes of the law.

LAVISH TIPPING

The man or woman who gives a waiter or a porter a tip that is entirely incommensurate with that individual's services, is not impressing by his generosity, but is earning the derision of the servants for his lack of *savoir faire*. Extravagance in tipping is like extravagance in any other form—it is decidedly vulgar.

A servant should be tipped according to the amount of service rendered. The hall-boy who brings you a pitcher of ice-water should not receive the same amount as the waiter who serves a full course dinner. Nor should the maid who cares for your room be forgotten while the porter who carries your trunks is handsomely rewarded for his few minutes' service.

IN DINING-ROOM OR DINING-CAR

At a hotel, when a guest expects to stay for a long time, he may reward the waiter in the dining-room for his services at the end of each week. One dollar is considered the

TIPPING 239

correct amount for a woman guest for a week's service in the dining-room, and one dollar and a half for the gentleman guest. Individual tips should amount to ten per cent. of the bill.

In the dining-car a tip of twenty-five cents is sufficient for the services rendered a man or woman. The woman who travels alone may leave twenty-five cents for the waiter in the dining-car. The man who travels alone should leave ten per cent. of the bill, or more according to the services received.

The woman who travels with children and stops at a hotel dining-room or a restaurant along the route, for dinner, should remember that children always require extra service and trouble, and the waiter or waitress should be tipped accordingly. A woman with one child should leave a twenty-five cent tip; and when there are more children the tip should be increased so as to be commensurate with the services received.

AT THE HOTEL

Women are never expected to tip as generously as men. At a hotel, the woman should remember the hall-boy, the chamber-maid, the porter, and the waiter in the dining-room. When her stay is a short one, twenty-five cents apiece is sufficient for each one, except the hall-boy, who is given a tip of ten cents whenever he performs an individual service. If her stay is longer, she should tip according to the amount of service received from each servant.

The man at the hotel is not expected to tip the chamber-maid unless she performs some very special service for him. But he tips all others who serve him in any way.

BOOK OF ETIQUETTE

The porter should receive ten cents for each trunk that he carries to the room, and more if he performs additional service. Ten cents is adequate compensation for the bell-boy whenever he performs some service, and it should be forthcoming immediately upon the completion of that service.

Both men and women guests are expected to tip a hotel employee whom they send out on an errand in proportion to the services rendered. If the trip to be taken is a long one, and entails a great deal of trouble. The tip should be a generous one.

THE TAXI-DRIVER

In large cities where taxicabs are fitted with meters that give the exact amount of ground covered and the corresponding cost, the traveler has nothing to fear. He may pay the amount with full confidence that he is not being over-charged. His tip should be fifteen or twenty-five cents, according to the length of the trip; or if the taxi-driver has been specially requested to make the trip in the shortest possible time, and if the distance covered is unusually long, a tip of fifty cents should be forth-coming.

But in some small towns where taxicabs have no meters, unsuspecting strangers are often forced to pay twice or even three times as much as the trip is actually worth. For this reason, it is always wise to know exactly the values of certain trips, and the careful man or woman will know when it is worth one dollar and when it is worth three. To remonstrate with the driver when you feel that he has excessively overcharged is to discourage his future attempts to do the same thing to others. A distance of twenty city blocks—or one mile—should never amount to

TIPPING 241

more than fifty cents; from this figure it should be easy to compute what longer trips should cost.

There is no more reason why exorbitant tips should be be paid the taxi-driver than the waiter. He performs no greater service, except in unusual cases, such as catching a train in time or getting you to a physician quickly. The amount of the tip should be in proportion to the amount of the bill, if the trip is just an ordinary one.

ON THE TRAIN

The man in the baggage room who gathers together and checks the trunks will expect a tip of at least twenty-five cents. A woman may offer less than this—but never less than ten cents. To the porter who carries the hand luggage aboard the train and finds a comfortable seat for the traveler, a tip of fifteen or twenty-five cents should be given, and the parlor car porter who performs many little services during the trip should be similarly tipped.

When the railroad journey is longer than twenty-four hours, the man and woman will find that they have several people to tip in the sleeper. The porter who makes the beds and blackens the boots will expect nothing less than twenty-five cents, and for extra service he is entitled to extra compensation. Others who perform services are tipped in amounts that are commensurate with the services rendered, and immediately upon the performance of those services.

CROSSING THE OCEAN

It was on a German steamship that the custom of raising a contribution for the band of musicians originated. Some steamships to-day still observe this custom, but on

242 BOOK OF ETIQUETTE

better ships, where the musicians are of a high order, it has been abolished. If the collection is made, at the end of the journey, each passenger should feel it incumbent upon him to contribute at least twenty-five cents. Fifty cents is not too much, and some people who have particularly enjoyed the music, offer one dollar or even more. It is very bad form, indeed, to refuse to contribute to this fund.

The servants to be remembered on the steamship are the bedroom steward, the table, deck and bathroom stewards, the stewardess, and the boy who blackens the boots. Masculine passengers do not tip the stewardess unless she has rendered them special service. Tips to the servants mentioned above should be governed by the amount of service rendered. For instance, if a woman passenger has been ill all the way across, she is expected to give a generous tip to the stewardess who has nursed her. Five dollars would not be considered extravagant in this case. The man who has been ill should be just as generous with the bedroom steward and all others who have attended him.

When leaving the ship, no one who has been of any service whatever should be forgotten. The porter who helps you with your hand luggage and sees you safely down the gang plank should be rewarded with no less than twenty-five cents.

TIPS IN FOREIGN COUNTRIES

Americans in Germany, England or France should learn at once the values of German, English and French money. Otherwise they may make mistakes that will cost them quite a bit. For instance, an American woman in Eng-

TIPPING 243

land recently gave a crown to a hotel maid, thinking that it was equivalent to our quarter. The maid realized that the woman did not know the value of it, and she explained it to her. But the traveler must remember that not all servants are so scrupulous.

Tips in foreign countries should be given on the same basis as the ones given to those who serve us here in America. Extravagance is bad form, and not to give at all is niggardly. The amount of the tip should always be commensurate with the service performed. Americans have every right to expect respectful and courteous treatment wherever they chance to be, and they must not feel that they are expected to pay exorbitant fees to obtain it.

CHAPTER IX

ETIQUETTE ABROAD

THE AMERICAN IN FOREIGN COUNTRIES

The American who goes abroad and expects to learn in a few days the customs, manners and even the language of the countries he visits, is like the proverbial Irishman who comes to America and expects to find the streets paved with gold. Both are doomed to disappointment.

One of the most undesirable features of travel abroad is to be forced to depend upon the half-incorrect interpretations of guides for one's comfort and pleasure. How much better it is to be able to talk to the natives of the country themselves, and to understand them and their ways! A little preliminary preparation before the trip, or while one is on the way, serves as an excellent foundation upon which to build one's knowledge of the language and customs of a foreign country.

Good manners are, of course, universal; and the man who is well-bred in America is sure to be correctly-mannered when he is in France or England. And yet there are slight differences between the etiquette of America and the etiquette of foreign countries. They do not affect one's courtesy or kindliness of manner, but they do affect those daily little conventionalities, such as greetings, farewells, table etiquette, addressing clergy and royalty, etc. To be ignorant of these rules is to be

244

ETIQUETTE ABROAD 245

susceptible to embarrassment and uncertainty, and to incur the displeasure and unfriendliness of foreigners of good social standing.

The following paragraphs will, we hope, help the man or woman who is traveling abroad, for they contain all the important details of foreign etiquette. But in addition, we have suggested that those who intend to visit France or Germany or any other foreign country, spend a little time reading about that country and learning a bit about the language. There are many good books available in public libraries and elsewhere, that teach one a great deal about the people, interesting places, and language of foreign countries.

ON ENGLISH SOIL

Perhaps it is because America and England have so much in common, that their etiquette is so very similar. We find that balls and receptions and entertainments, dinners, calls, funerals and weddings, in fact, almost all social functions are celebrated in practically the same manner as is considered best form here in America. The changes are so slight that they are not important enough to mention.

But there is one radical difference between English and American conventionalities that usually cause difficulty to the tourist. We refer to the royal society of England which requires a very special kind of recognition. The traveling American who visits an English court will expose himself to a great deal of embarrassment if he does not know the correct court etiquette—if he does not know the proper titles and their recognition, how to address the King or Queen, how to conduct himself while in the presence of royalty.

BOOK OF ETIQUETTE

ADDRESSING ROYALTY

Although every American tourist delights in being presented at court, or to a royal personage, it is usually regarded as a nervous and embarrassing business—for the reason that one does not quite know just what is correct to say and do. When addressing the King, there are two correct forms and no others that may be used. One may say either, "Your Majesty" or "Sir" There are also two forms that may be used when addressing the Queen. They are, "Your Majesty" or "Madame." When answering a question put by either of these rulers, one may not use the brief "No" or "Yes." "No, madame," or "Yes, sir," are the correct forms. When addressing the King, the form "Your Majesty" is used.

All children of the King and Queen are addressed as "Your Royal Highness." This same title is used when addressing the brother or sister of the reigning monarchs, or the brother or sister of the late King. In speaking to royalty, one does not use the simple expression "you," but expresses oneself in this manner, "Has your Royal Highness been to America recently?"

One rule that all Americans should observe when in the presence of foreign royalty is to wait until they are addressed by the persons of rank. They themselves should not volunteer remarks but should enter into the conversation only when they are directly addressed. To use a title of rank, such as "Your Majesty" or "Your Royal Highness" incessantly, is to make it seem superficial. It should be used only when respect and convention demand it.

When presented to royalty, a man is expected to bow,

ETIQUETTE ABROAD 247

a woman to courtesy. The hand is never offered in greeting, unless the person of rank makes the first motion. In the presence of the Queen everyone should show some mark of respect—men stand with heads uncovered and women bow slightly. Americans should follow these customs if they do not wish to earn the enmity of their English brothers and make their stay in the country unpleasant. But most of all, they should do it because it is the *polite* and *proper* thing to do. Americans should also remain standing at the theater or opera when the national anthem, "God Save the Queen," is sung, or while the rest of the audience stands in respect for a member of the royal family who has not yet been seated.

OTHER ENGLISH TITLES

An American in England is very likely to meet some persons of high hereditary title, if they are not presented at the court itself. When speaking of a Duke, one says, "The Duke of Lancastershire." When addressing him, one says, "Your Grace" or "My Lord Duke." Familiarly, by those who know him well and address him as an equal, the Duke is addressed merely as "Duke." The same rule applies to the Duchess. Formally she is addressed as "Your Grace"; familiarly she is addressed as "Duchess."

The eldest son is entitled to the highest of the lesser titles of his father. Thus, the eldest son of a Duke who was a Marquis immediately before receiving his ducal degree, is known as the Marquis, and is addressed as "Lord Barrie" (if Barrie happened to be the surname of the family). Earls, Viscounts and Barons are addressed in the same manner, when their titles are

248 BOOK OF ETIQUETTE

given them as courtesies, as the eldest sons of Dukes.

The wife of anyone of the titled men mentioned above would be addressed as "Lady Barrie." A curt "No" or "Yes" is extremely rude on the part of an American when answering a question put by the wife of a person of nobility. One should say, "No, Lady Barrie."

The younger sons of a Duke are addressed as "Lord James" or "Lord Sidney Barrie." Daughters are addressed as "Lady Helen" or "Lady Louise Barrie."

A Marquis (not the eldest son of a Duke, but a recognized Marquis by English law) is entitled to the formal title of "My Lord" or "Your Lordship" when addressed by traveling Americans—or by their own country-people. By his friends or equals he is addressed as "Lord Denbigh" or "Marquis." On formal occasions, or by those of lesser rank, a Marchioness is addressed as "My Lady" or "Your Ladyship." But her friends and equals call her "Lady Penhope" or "Marchioness."

Just as the eldest son of a Duke bears a "courtesy title," so does the eldest son of a Marquis. This eldest son is called "Lord Denbigh." The daughters of the Marquis are "Lady Helen" or "Lady Janet," and they are addressed in this manner by their friends and equals. Formally, an Earl is addressed as "My Lord" or "Your Lordship." The wife of an Earl is formally addressed as is the Marchioness. But by her intimate friends and her social equals she is addressed as "Countess" or "Lady Hendrick."

The eldest son of an Earl bears his father's second title. There are no titles for the younger sons of an Earl. His daughters are addressed in the same manner as are the daughters of a Marquis. A Viscount is addressed formally as "My Lord" and his friends and equals

ETIQUETTE ABROAD 249

address him familiarly as "Lord Roberts." In addressing the wife of a Viscount, one uses the same forms outlined for the wife of an Earl. The sons and daughters of a Viscount, when addressed or spoken about, are referred to as Mr. or Miss Roberts, but when formally introduced, this form is used, "The Honorable Henry Roberts."

—AND STILL OTHER TITLES

The American traveler in England will certainly have a great many titles to remember, especially if he expects to mingle to any extent with the royal society. There are still others besides those outlined above. The following are "lesser" titles, but are used perhaps even more frequently than those given in the preceding paragraphs.

There are the Baron and Baroness, for instance, who are addressed respectively as "My Lord" and "Your Ladyship." Their children have the same titular rank and are addressed in the same manner. The Baronet is addressed formally and familiarly as "Sir Thomas" without the addition of his surname. His title is really only an hereditary privilege. But his wife enjoys the title of "Lady Merick" or "Lady Carol," instead of just "Lady Sylvia." The children of a Baronet have no title.

A Knight is addressed as "Lord Henry" or "Lord James," both formally and familiarly. His wife is addressed in the same form as that used for the wife of a Baronet. The children of a Knight are called merely Mr. or Miss.

ADDRESSING CLERGY ABROAD

Another difficulty that often confronts the stranger in England, is that of correctly addressing the clergy.

250 BOOK OF ETIQUETTE

England is a land of titles, and to be at ease one must know how to place each title properly and pay proper respect where it is due.

In England the Archbishops of Canterbury and York and all the bishops (with the exception of two) are called "Lords Spiritual." They enjoy the privilege of sitting in the House of Lords. Thus, when addressing them formally, the form "Your Grace" should be used. "Archbishop" may be used only by those who are addressing that dignitary familiarly as a friend or an equal. Bishops should be formally addressed as "Your Lordship" or "My Lord," but merely as "Bishop" by their friends. Their wives, and the wives of archbishops, have no title, nor do the children of either archbishop or bishop have any title other than Mr. or Miss.

Following the bishop in rank, comes the Dean, addressed simply as "Dean Harris." His wife is known only as "Mrs. Harris." The same forms apply to the Archdeacon and his wife. Other clergymen—canons, vicars, rectors and curates—have no titles and are addressed simply as "Mr. Brown" or "Mr. Smith" as the case may be.

LAWYERS, STATESMEN AND OFFICIALS—HOW TO ADDRESS THEM

While traveling about in merry England, one may find it necessary to seek legal advice or the protection of a court. The etiquette is slightly different from that observed in America.

The members of the judiciary, for instance, are not spoken of as "Judge Brown" and "Judge Harris," but as "Mr. Justice Brown" and "Mr. Justice Harris." While

ETIQUETTE ABROAD 251

presiding in his court, the member of the judiciary is addressed as "My Lord," "Your honor," "Your worship," according to the position occupied. In private life, however, he is plain "Mr. Smith."

Whether addressed formally or familiarly, the members of the Cabinet, and the prime minister are simply Mr. Blank, unless they have titles conferred upon them by the King or inherited. In this case they use their titles constantly and are addressed accordingly.

The Lord Mayor of London is entitled to the honorary title of "His Lordship." He may also be addressed as "My Lord Mayor" at social gatherings.

AT THE COURT OF ENGLAND

The social activities of the English Court, and the etiquette governing these activities, should be known and thoroughly understood by every American who ever intends to visit that country. The war interfered slightly with the functions of the court, but with the return to normal these have been resumed with all their pre-war ceremony.

Usually four Courts are held every season, two in the early part of spring, and two at equal intervals later on. This may be altered, however, to suit conditions; as, for instance, in Nineteen-Fourteen there were only three Courts, and in Nineteen-Fifteen there were none at all.

American women who wish to be presented at Court may either be presented by the wife of the American Ambassador or by some English woman of title and position who has herself been received by the Queen. The American Ambassador has the privilege of sending to the authorities in whose hands the matter rests, the names of

252 BOOK OF ETIQUETTE

several American women suitable for presentation at
Court. Those who wish this privilege, should register
their names at the offices of the Embassy in London, sufficiently ahead of time for due consideration.

In addition to the registering of her name at the Embassy, the woman who wishes to be presented at Court
should bring to the Ambassador a letter of recommendation from some member of the American government who
is well known to the Ambassador. Then, if the application is accepted, her name and credentials will be sent to
Buckingham Palace, from whence invitations will be issued if the Ambassador's list is approved.

Having gained the coveted invitation to appear at the
Court of Her Majesty, the Queen, the American woman
must be careful that she knows exactly what to wear.

WHAT TO WEAR TO COURT

Before attempting to appear at Court, the American
woman should consult a reliable modiste. She will be
able to tell her exactly the correct thing to wear at her
presentation.

Court gowns invariably have trains, and the head dress
is always elaborate. The dress itself must be fashioned
according to the style of the moment, and in this the
woman must be guided by her dressmaker. For a young,
unmarried woman a dress of thin, light-colored material
is suggested, unadorned by jewels of any kind. The
matron may wear diamonds or pearls, but must not attempt to emulate the gaudiness of a Queen Elizabeth.

The well-bred woman will not feel awkward in the vast
room where all the great personages are assembled. She
will learn beforehand, just how to enter the room, how to

ETIQUETTE ABROAD 253

kiss the Queen's hand and how to conduct herself with poise and grace during the period of presentation.

THE KING'S LEVÉES

The American gentleman who wishes to be presented to His Majesty, may arrange through his Ambassador to attend one of the levées which the King holds at St. James' Palace. These levées are not quite as ceremonious as the Courts which the Queen holds, but they require a certain definite etiquette which must not be overlooked.

For instance, the American who is not in uniform, must wear the correct dress prescribed for the occasion. It is known as levée dress, and a competent London tailor will be able to inform the American gentleman of just what it consists. He must not attempt to appear at the levée in any other than these conventional clothes. Slight variations take place in these levée costumes, from time to time, and the American in England should make sure by consulting with a fashionable tailor.

It is wise also, before attending a levée, to have a little chat with a friend or acquaintance who has already attended one, and learn from him the correct way to conduct oneself throughout the presentation.

IN FRANCE

France is a land of polished manners. Here one is either cultured or uncultured. Mistakes in etiquette, divergence from the path of good form, are not tolerated in good society. The American in France must know

254 BOOK OF ETIQUETTE

exactly what is correct to do and say in that country, if he wishes to enjoy his visit.

The brief expressions "Yes" or "No" are never used in France when one wishes to be polite. It must be followed by the correct title, such as "Yes, Monsieur" or "No, Madame" In the morning, upon greeting an acquaintance, no matter how slightly you know him, it is correct to say, "Bonjour, Monsieur." When expressing thanks for a courtesy or for requested information, one says, "Merci, Madame." And the customary farewell is "Au revoir, Mademoiselle."

Politeness is universal in France. One greets shop clerks as cordially as one greets one's best friend. Upon entering the French shop one should say "Bonjour, Monsieur" to the floorwalker, and "Bonjour, Madame" to the saleslady. In the restaurant it is proper to say "Merci, Monsieur," to the head waiter who shows you to your place. The waiters are adddressed as *garçon*, but the waitresses are called *Madame* or *Mademoiselle*.

If one happens to brush against someone accidentally, or to get into someone's way, it is very important that polite apologies be offered. To hurry on without so much as saying, "Pardon, Monsieur," is extremely rude, and Frenchmen are quick to notice it. They are very courteous and they expect visitors to be the same.

ADDRESSING TITLED PEOPLE IN FRANCE

"Monsieur le Comte" is the correct mode of address to employ towards a Count in France. A Baron is addressed as "Monsieur le Baron." His wife, however, is called simply "Madame —— "

Officers in the Army are addressed in the following man-

ETIQUETTE ABROAD 255

ner: "Mon Capitaine," "Mon Général," etc. It is a decided breach of good conduct to address an officer in the French army as "Monsieur," especially when he is in uniform. When speaking about a certain officer, one may say, "Le Général Denbigh."

The concierge and his wife are known merely as Monsieur and Madame. The parish priest, however, is spoken of and to as, "Monsieur le curé." A nun is addressed always as "Ma Sœur."

Be careful not to forget the correct forms of address in France, for Frenchmen are quick to take offence and much ill-will may unwittingly be incurred by the American man or woman who does not pay proper respect where it is due, who does not use the correct titles at the correct time. And the American traveler in France should remember that his manners and conduct in that country reflect not only upon his own manners and breeding, but upon the manners and customs of the country he represents.

CERTAIN FRENCH CONVENTIONS

In France the first recognition of acquaintanceship must come from the gentleman. For instance, if a young American man makes the acquaintance of a young French woman, she will expect him to raise his hat when they meet again, before she nods to him. In America it is the reverse—the young lady has the privilege of acknowledging or ignoring an acquaintanceship.

Not only must the hat be raised to women, in France, but to men also. A young American and a young Frenchman who are known to each other raise their hats simultaneously when they encounter each other on the

BOOK OF ETIQUETTE

street. But when the Frenchman is the elder of the two, or the more distinguished, the American is expected to wait until he makes the first motion of recognition.

The American who stops at a small hotel in France for a period of two days or more, should feel it his duty to nod courteously to every woman guest of the hotel he chances to meet, whether or not she is a total stranger. This is considered a conventional courtesy which all well-bred people in France observe. However, it does not serve the purpose of an introduction, and the American must not make the mistake of thinking that this privilege entitles him to address the women guests without the introduction of a mutual friend or acquaintance.

Frenchmen always stand with heads uncovered when a funeral passes, and women bow for a moment. The well-bred American man and woman in France will also observe this custom. Nor will they neglect to remain standing while the *Marsellaise* is being sung

DINNER ETIQUETTE

An invitation to dine should be accepted or declined promptly when one is visiting in France. And one may not decline unless one has a very good excuse, such as having a previous engagement, or being called away on the day set for the dinner.

It is considered polite to arrive twenty minutes or a half-hour before dinner is served. If it is a formal and elaborate dinner, evening dress should be worn; but afternoon or semi-evening dress is appropriate for the informal dinner. It is not at all incorrect, if one is in doubt, to ask the host or hostess whether one should wear full dress or not. It is certainly wiser than to make oneself

ETIQUETTE ABROAD 257

conspicuous by wearing different dress from all the other guests.

In France, the order in which the guests proceed to dinner is as follows: the host leads the way with the woman guest of honor, or the most distinguished woman guest, on his arm. Directly behind him follows the hostess on the arm of the masculine guest to be honored; and they are followed by the other guests, who proceed arm in arm.

According to the latest dinner etiquette in France, coffee is served for both the men and women at the dinner table. But when the dinner is very large and fashionable, it is still customary for the women to retire to the drawing-room, where the hostess presides over the coffee-urn. When men and women leave the dining-room together, they resume the same order as they observed when they entered it.

The American who is a guest at a formal dinner in France should pay a call upon the hostess within a week's time. This call is known as the *"visite de digestion."*

FRENCH WEDDING ETIQUETTE

Weddings are occasions of solemn dignity in every country, but in France they are perhaps more dignified than anywhere else. Here no rice and old shoes are cast after the bride and bridegroom—it would be considered a most shocking thing to do. Good wishes, politely expressed, are the only good-by offerings of friends and relatives.

There are usually two ceremonies to be celebrated at the French wedding—first the civil, and later the religious, marriage. At the civil wedding, which is held two or three days before the religious ceremony, only a few intimate

BOOK OF ETIQUETTE

friends and relatives of the two families are present. But the ceremony at church is a very important affair and all friends and acquaintances of both families are invited to attend. Those who cannot attend should send cards of regret to the bride's parents.

BALLS

Very elaborate and gay indeed are the balls of France. There is, for instance, the *bals blancs,* at which all ladies are gowned in pure white and only maidens and bachelors are expected to be present. Men guests at the *bal blanc* wear the conventional evening dress.

At a ball in France, a gentleman may request to dance with a lady without having first been introduced to her. Even a total stranger may approach a lady on the ball-room floor and ask for a dance. But it is considered very bad form for a young man and woman to "sit out" a dance together or retire to the veranda or lawn.

ABOUT CALLS AND CARDS

If one expects to remain in France any length of time at all, it is important that one know and understand the etiquette of calls and cards in that country.

Calls are paid just as frequently in France as they are in America. Between two and six o'clock in the afternoon is the correct time for calling in the former country. One observes very much the same conventions of calling that one does here in America, except that the gentleman wears both his gloves when entering a drawing-room, and that the hostess does not rise to welcome a masculine caller. (However, the French hostess always does rise to greet

ETIQUETTE ABROAD 259

an elderly gentleman, a distinguished person, or a member of the clergy.)

French introductions are never haphazard, never careless. The hostess introduces freely all the guests that assemble in her home, but she is not, as the American hostess sometimes is, careless and hurried. In acknowledging an introduction, a brief, polite greeting should be expressed; French people rarely shake hands.

The significance of the bent visiting card still remains in France, though here in America it has been almost entirely eliminated. When a hostess finds the card of a friend or acquaintance, with one of its corners turned down, she knows that that friend called for the purpose of a visit but found no one at home. In fact, that is almost the only time when cards are left in France—when the person called upon is not at home. However, a dinner call is often paid by the simple process of card-leaving.

CORRESPONDENCE

The French people are very particular in their correspondence. Certain set rules of salutation and closing are observed, and the margins themselves have a particular significance. For instance, when writing a letter to a French person, a wide margin should be left on the left side of the sheet; and the greater the social prestige and distinction of the person addressed, the wider this margin must be.

A man writing to another man who is an intimate friend begins his letter in this manner: "Mon cher Frederick," or "Mon cher ami." The closing to this letter would be, "Bien à vous," or "Bien cordialement à vous." When the two men are not intimate friends, a letter should begin,

260 BOOK OF ETIQUETTE

"Cher Monsieur," or "Mon cher Monsieur Blank," and should end with "Croyez à mes sentiments dévoués." Strangers address each other merely as "Monsieur," and close with "Recevez je vous prie l'assurance de ma consideration distinguée."

When writing to a woman friend, a man begins his letter with "Chère Madame et ami," or "Chère Mademoiselle." But when he is a stranger or just a slight acquaintance, he begins his letter with "Madame" and concludes it with "Veuillez, Madame, reçevoir l'expression de tout mon respect." The French have very pretty expressions of greeting and conclusion, and they expect every well-bred person to use them.

A woman writing to a gentleman addresses him in the following manner, if he is an intimate friend: "Monsieur," or "Cher Monsieur Brown," and she closes the letter with the courtesy phrase, "Agrèez, cher monsieur, l'expression de mes sentiments d'amitie." Greetings and closings are more formal when the woman addresses a masculine stranger or slight acquaintance by letter. She begins simply with "Monsieur," and closes with, "Veuillez, monsieur, reçevoir l'expression de mes sentiments distingués."

Special forms of address and conclusion are used when writing officers in the French army. A general or commander are addressed in the following manner: "Monsieur le général," or "Monsieur le commandant." The letter should be couched in terms of most exact respect. Tradespeople in France are addressed by letter in the following manner: "Monsieur C.," or "Madame C.," and the conclusion should be, "Agreez, Monsieur C., mes civilités." A servant should be addressed with "Je prie M. Smith (or Mad. Smith) de vouloir bien."

In France abbreviations on the envelope are considered

ETIQUETTE ABROAD 261

very bad form. M. may never be used for Monsieur, nor may Mlle. be used for Mademoiselle. The full title and name must appear on the envelope.

THE AMERICAN IN GERMANY

The American who finds himself in Germany for the first time is likely to be puzzled and embarrassed by the numerous different manners and customs in each little town and duchy. What is correct in one place, may be incorrect elsewhere. Thus it is impossible to give certain rules of etiquette to be followed by the American in the German Empire. He must be guided by good judgment and by the advice of his German friends.

However, one may be certain of one thing—throughout the length and breadth of the German empire the greatest ceremony is observed in correspondence of all kinds. As great courtesy and respect is paid the stranger as the friend. When writing to a man or woman of social distinction, this impressive inscription appears on the envelope and begins the letter: "To the high and well-born Mrs. Robert Smith." It sounds, perhaps, a trifle crude in the English, but in the native German it is a pretty and courteous phrase and a true expression of respect.

When writing to a person of lesser social importance, as a business letter, for instance, one should begin with "Honored Sir." The expression, "Lieber Freund," should be used only when writing informally to a dear friend. In fact, the same method of address as is used in writing English letters may be used when writing to friends and acquaintances in Germany.

The hours for paying calls and leaving cards differ in

262   BOOK OF ETIQUETTE

the various localities. Ordinarily, the correct time would be between half-past three and half-past four o'clock in the afternoon, although in some localities calls are not considered correct before five o'clock. In Germany, card-leaving should be followed in the same manner as card-leaving in the United States.

When meeting a feminine acquaintance in Germany, the American gentleman does not wait for recognition to come from her, but immediately bows and raises his hat. As in France, he may request a lady to dance with him, at a ball, without having first requested an introduction. And also, as in France, it is considered polite to bow and raise one's hat to the ladies who are at the same hotel, although here again, the privilege does not serve as an introduction.

At all times, men and women in Germany should be given full recognition of their titles and positions. A German woman always enjoys the title bestowed upon her husband. The wife of a general expects to be addressed as "Mrs. General Blank,' and the wife of a doctor should be called "Mrs. Doctor Blank." Men of official or professional rank and titles are addressed as, "Mr. Professor, Mr. General, Mr. Doctor, etc." "Herr Doktor Smith" is the correct German form—and to omit the *Herr* is a breach of good conduct.

THE PERFECT AMERICAN TOURIST

Unfortunately, there are some Americans who go abroad each year merely because it is the "fashion" to do so, and because they wish to impress their friends and acquaintances at home with their social distinction and importance. These people are wont to let their money talk for them— instead of their manners. But there are many things that

ETIQUETTE ABROAD 263

wealth will not excuse; and among them is lack of courtesy and breeding.

The American abroad, whether he is traveling for pastime, pleasure or business, should remember primarily that he is a representative of the United States, and that as such he owes his country the duty of making his manners a polished reflection of the manners of all Americans. He must be courteous, polite, kind, *gentlemanly*. He must conform with the customs of the country he chances to be in, and he must avoid all suggestion of superiority on his part, or disdain for the customs of the other country.

There is a certain fellow-feeling, a certain sympathy and kindliness that can take the place of conventionalities when one is not sure of the customs of certain countries. Perhaps you do not know the French language, and you wish to have a window raised while you are traveling on a French railroad. Is it forgivable to bend across a man or woman and raise the window without a word of excuse, or a cordial smile of understanding? And yet how often do we see this thing done! Many a seemingly well-bred man or woman will raise the window next to another man or woman without so much as asking permission to do so! The proper thing to do when one does not know the language, is to smile in a cordial manner to the person or persons in the vicinity of the window, indicate that you would like to have it raised, and wait until your request is understood and granted before you venture to raise it. Then a polite "Merci," which means "Thank you," and which everyone should know and remember, should be given.

It is not always easy to do and say what is absolutely correct when one is in a strange country among people who speak a strange language. But he who is kind and

264 BOOK OF ETIQUETTE

courteous at all times, who has a ready smile and a polished manner, will avoid much of the embarrassment that awaits the tourist who is indifferent and careless. The proverb, "All doors open to courtesy," is as true in France and England as it is in America.

APPENDIX

FOREIGN WORDS IN FREQUENT SOCIAL USAGE

Ad infinitum, L., to infinity.

À la carte, Fr., according to the bill of fare at table.

À la mode, Fr., according to the mode or fashion.

À la Russe, Fr., according to the Russian fashion (individual portions).

A propos, L., to the point.

Au fait, Fr., well-versed in social custom.

Au revoir, Fr., good-by till we meet again.

Ben educato, It., well educated.

Billet d'amour, Fr., love letter.

Blasé, Fr., world-weary.

Bona fide, L., in good faith.

Bonbonnière, Fr., bonbon dish.

Bon jour, Fr., good morning; good day.

Bon ton, Fr., fashionable society.

Bon voyage, Fr., good journey to you.

Bouillion, Fr., a clear broth.

Boutonnière, Fr., a flower for the buttonhole.

Buffet, Fr., a sideboard for china, silver or glass.

Carte blanche, Fr., unconditional permission.

Chancel, L., space in church reserved for the officiating clergy.

Chère amie, Fr., dear friend (fem.).

BOOK OF ETIQUETTE

Coiffure, Fr., dressing of the hair.

Collation, Fr., a light repast.

Compotiers, Fr., dish for served stewed fruits or bonbons.

Corsage bouquet, Fr., flowers fastened on bodice.

Cortège, Fr., a formal procession.

Coterie, Fr., a social set; a clique.

Cotillon, Fr., a dance for four couples.

Coup d'ètat, Fr., a sudden decisive blow in politics.

Débutante, Fr., a young lady just introduced to society.

Décolleté, Fr., fashionably low-cut for evening wear.

De luxe, Fr., of luxury; made with unusual elegance.

Dénouement, Fr., the issue.

Dramatis personæ, L., characters in the play.

De trop, Fr., too much, too many.

Demoiselle, Fr., young lady.

Éclat, Fr., renown, glory.

Élite, Fr., better society.

En buffet, Fr., served from the buffet; no tables.

En déshabille, Fr., in undress; négligée.

En masse, Fr., in a mass.

En route, Fr., on the way.

En suite, Fr., in company.

En toilette, Fr., in full dress.

Entrée, Fr., a side-dish, served as one course of a meal.

Entre nous, Fr., between ourselves.

Ensemble, Fr., all together.

E pluribus unum, L., one out of many.

Et cetera, L., and everything of the sort.

Et tu, Brute, L., and thou also, Brutus.

Eureka, Gr., I have found it.

Fète, Fr., a festive social occasion.

Fète champêtre, Fr., an open-air festival or entertainment.

APPENDIX 267

Filets mignon, **Fr.,** small pieces of beef tenderloin, served with sauce.

Finesse, Fr., social art in its highest conception.

Fondant, Fr., soft icing or glacé.

Finis, Fr., the end.

Garçon, Fr., boy.

Grace à Dieu, Fr., grace of God.

Hors d'œuvre, Fr., out of course; special course.

In memorium, L., to the memory of.

Le beau monde, Fr., the fashionable world.

Lettre de cachet, Fr., a sealed letter.

Ma chère, Fr., my dear (fem.).

Mal de mer, Fr., sea-sickness.

Mardi gras, Fr., Shrove Tuesday.

Mayonnaise, Fr., a salad sauce of egg, oil, vinegar and spices beaten together.

Menu, **Fr.,** bill of table fare.

Mon ami, Fr., my friend (mon amie, fem.).

Musicale, **Fr.,** private concert.

Négligée, Fr., morning dress; easy, loose dress.

Noblesse oblige, **Fr.,** rank imposes obligations; much is expected from one in good position.

Nom de plume, Fr., an assumed name of a writer.

Notre Dame, Fr., Our Lady.

O Temporal O Mores! L., Oh the times! Oh the manners!

Passé, Fr., out of date.

Penchant, Fr., a strong or particular liking.

Pièce de résistance, Fr., something substantial by way of entertainment; most substantial course of a dinner; literally, a piece of resistance (a main event or incident).

Pour prendre congé, **Fr.,** to depart, take leave. (P.p.c. on

268 BOOK OF ETIQUETTE

calling cards meaning the departure of a caller for a long voyage, hence a parting call.)

Prima donna, Ital., the chief woman vocalist of a concert.

Pro patria, L., for our country.

Protégée, Fr., under the protection of another.

Rendezvous, Fr., an appointed place for a meeting.

R.s.v.p., Fr., (Repondez s'il vous plàit), please reply.

Requiescat in pace, L., may he (she) rest in peace.

Résumé, Fr., a summary or abstract.

Salon, Fr., a drawing-room; the room where guests are received.

Sang froid, Fr., coolness, indifference.

Sans souci, Fr., without care.

Savoir faire, Fr., knowledge of social customs; tact.

Table à manger, Fr., dining-table.

Table d'hôte, Fr., a public dinner at hotel or restaurant

Trousseau, Fr., the bridal outfit.

Tout de suite, Fr., immediately.

Tout ensemble, Fr., all together.

Veni, Vidi, Viei, L., I came, I saw, I conquered.

Verbatim, L., word for word.

Vis-à-vis, Fr., face-to-face.

Voilà, Fr., behold; there you are!